NO
SELF
NO
PROBLEM

NO
SELF
NO
PROBLEM

How Neuropsychology Is
Catching Up to **BUDDHISM**

CHRIS NIEBAUER, Ph.D.

Hier⊕phantpublishing

Cover design by Emma Smith
Cover art by: Brain image by Eli Deitch | Shutterstock
Buddha image by Mirinae | Shutterstock
Photo of Brad Pitt by s_bukley | Shutterstock
Illustrations by Garylarts
Interior Design by Frame25 Productions

Hierophant Publishing
www.hierophantpublishing.com

If you are unable to order this book from your local bookseller,
you may order directly from the publisher.

Library of Congress Control Number: 2019943287

ISBN: 978-1-938289-97-2

10 9 8 7 6 5 4 3 2

Printed on acid-free paper in the United States.

Table of Contents

For one who has conquered the mind, the mind is the best of friends; but for one who has failed to do so, his mind will remain the greatest enemy.

—Bhagavad Gita

Preface

My interest in psychology and the inner workings of the mind began after the death of my father when I was twenty years old. The impact of this event was profound, and the deep suffering I experienced led me to study the mechanics of mind with the goal of helping myself and others. I believed that if there were a way into this mess, there had to be some way out, and I was set on finding it. At the time, most everybody was sure that the secrets of the mind would be found in the brain. Our species has long debated the nature of the relationship between the mind and brain, and I think about it like this: The brain is the subject and the mind is the verb, or as cognitive scientist Marvin Minsky put it, "The mind is what the brain does."

There were many people looking to identify how the mind worked via the brain at the time. In fact, this topic became so popular that Congress even declared the 1990s the "Decade of the Brain." Thinking that this path might hold some promise as a way out of mental suffering, I finished a Ph.D. in cognitive neuropsychology in 1996.

Neuropsychology is the study of the architecture of the brain and how that architecture relates to how we experience the world, specifically our thoughts and the resulting behavior. Neuropsychology has successfully mapped certain processes onto specific brain areas. From facial recognition to empathy, neuropsychology can now place specific processes and brain functions precisely at specific locations on the neural landscape.

Of course, none of this mattered to me at the time of my father's death. All I knew was that I was suffering, and my hope was that the secret to ending that suffering, or at least to understanding it, could be found in the mechanics of the brain. Yet despite countless hours spent in the classroom, I wasn't finding any real answers regarding the issue.

So I turned to the teachings of the East, and it was here that I began to find what I felt was missing from the traditional psychological approach. I also began to notice striking parallels between specific findings on the brain and the ideas expressed in Buddhism, Taoism, and other schools of Eastern thought. As I finished my graduate work in a lab that studied the differences between the left and right brain, I split my time between the different needs of those two halves with day-to-day life as a student of science for my left brain and weekend retreats on Eastern philosophy that seemed to fulfill my right brain.

While in graduate school, I marveled at the shift that had been taking place in the field of physics.[1] Several researchers had noticed the similarities between the findings of quantum mechanics and the teachings of the East. I remember going into a professor's office and with the joy of a kid on Christmas morning sharing that what was being discovered in physics confirmed what had been said in the East long ago. To my great disappointment, the professor came right out and said that there was no Santa; he attributed the similarities in these new findings to simple coincidence.

Despite his dismissal, I never lost hope that a connection between neuroscience and Eastern thought would be realized. In the late 1990s, I would have bet I was one of very few professors who offered a class on Zen and the brain. However, just a few years later the Dalai Lama was invited to be the lead speaker at a major conference in neuroscience, and today the notion that neuroscience and Eastern philosophy can complement each other is practically a genre of its own.[2]

Now, scientists and academics have documented the many positive effects of the practices of the East. Take meditation, which we now know improves attention.[3] Harvard neuroscientist Sara Lazar has shown that long-term meditators have a thicker cortex—the area of the brain that specializes in high-level decision-making. This wrinkled outer layer of the brain is made up of neurons, which are information-processing cells. It has been well established that the cortex in general shrinks with age; however, Lazar found that the effect of regular meditation on the cortex was so profound that fifty-year-old meditators had a prefrontal cortex that looked like that of a twenty-five-year-old. Even an eight-week mindfulness-based stress reduction program had a significant impact on the brain. Those doing the mindfulness program had smaller amygdalae—the aggressive part of the brain that reacts to stress—and larger temporoparietal junctions (TPJs), a part of the brain associated with empathy and compassion.[4]

Similar astonishing effects have been found as a result of tai chi, a form of movement-based meditation. The promising effects of tai chi range from the physical (for example, lower blood pressure) to the mental (enhanced cognitive function).[5] The ancient Hindu practice of yoga has also yielded similar findings.[6] For example, Dr. Chantal Villemure, a researcher at the

National Center for Complementary and Alternative Medicine in Bethesda, Maryland, has found that areas of the cortex were larger for those who practiced yoga.[7] This research even supported findings that the section of the brain that stores memory—the hippocampus—was larger for those practicing yoga.

David Creswell at Carnegie Mellon has shown that a simple three-day retreat on mindfulness meditation can change the brain and lower inflammation.[8] Those in the mindfulness group had a reduced level of a biomarker for inflammation linked to diseases such as diabetes, arthritis, and cancer. In fact, it is difficult to find research uncovering a negative effect—or even no effect at all—from practicing these ancient arts of the East.

These studies are wonderfully informative, yet I believe the research done by many in the West points to something even more profound than the physical and mental benefits of adopting Eastern practices. For the first time in history, the findings of scientists in the West strongly support, in many cases without meaning to, one of the most fundamental insights of the East: that the individual self is more akin to a fictional character than a real thing.

In other words, the self that you think you know *is not real*.

We do not yet understand the full implication of these studies or their impact on Western ideas of what it means to be human. This book aims to dive into that process by examining those studies, weighing their significance, and understanding what they ask of us.

No Self, No Problem

Introduction

Stop thinking, and end your problems.
—Lao Tzu, The Tao Te Ching
(Stephen Mitchell translation)

Who are we? Why are we here? Why do we suffer?

Humans have grappled with these questions since time immemorial. Philosophers, spiritual leaders, scientists, and artists have all weighed in on them. In Western philosophy, the best answer to the question of who we are is that *thinking* is the defining characteristic of humanity. There is no more concise example of this than philosopher René Descartes' famous statement *cogito, ergo sum*, or, "I think, therefore I am."

This reverence for thinking is in stark contrast to the tenets of Eastern philosophy found in traditions such as Buddhism, Taoism, and certain schools of Hinduism. These traditions at best advocate a distrust of the thinking mind and often go further to claim that the thinking mind is part of the problem rather than the solution. Zen Buddhism offers us the saying, "No thought, no problem."

The brain-powered individual, which is variously called the self, the ego, the mind, or "me," lies at the center of Western thought. In the worldview of the West, we herald the greatest thinkers as world-changers. But who is this? Let's take a closer look at the thinker, or the "me," we all take for granted. This definition will be essential throughout our discussion.

This "I" is for most of us the first thing that pops into our minds when we think about who we are. The "I" represents the idea of our individual self, the one that sits between the ears and behind the eyes and is "piloting" the body. The "pilot" is in charge, it doesn't change very much, and it feels to us like the thing that brings our thoughts and feelings to life. It observes, makes decisions, and carries out actions—just like the pilot of an airplane.

This I/ego is what we think of as our true selves, and this individual self is the experiencer and the controller of things like thoughts, feelings, and actions. The pilot self feels like it is running the show. It is stable and continuous. It is also in control of our physical body; for example, this self understands that it is "my body." But unlike our physical body, it does not perceive itself as changing, ending (except, perhaps for atheists, in bodily death), or being influenced by anything other than itself.

Now let's turn to the East. Buddhism, Taoism, the Advaita Vedanta school of Hinduism, and other schools of Eastern thought have quite a different take on the self, the ego, or "me." They say that this idea of "me" is a fiction, although a very convincing one. Buddhism has a word for this concept—*anatta*, which is often translated as "no self"—which is one of the most fundamental tenets of Buddhism, if not *the* most important.

This idea sounds radical, even nonsensical, to those who are trained in Western traditions. It seems to contradict our everyday experience, indeed our whole sense of being.

This book will explore strong evidence suggesting that the concept of the self is simply a construct of the mind, rather than a physical thing located somewhere within the brain itself. Put another way, it is the process of thinking that creates the self, rather than there being a self having any independent existence separate from thought. The self is more like a verb than a noun. To take it a step further, the implication is that without thought, the self does not, in fact, exist. It's as if contemporary neuroscience and psychology are just now catching up with what Buddhism, Taoism, and Advaita Vedanta Hinduism have been teaching for over 2,500 years.

This may be a difficult point to grasp, chiefly because we've mistaken the *process* of thinking as a genuine *thing* for so long. It will take some time to see the idea of a "me" as simply an idea rather than a fact. Your illusionary self—the voice in your head—is very convincing. It narrates the world, determines your beliefs, replays your memories, identifies with your physical body, manufactures your projections of what might happen in the future, and creates your judgments about the past. It is this sense of self that we feel from the moment we open our eyes in the morning to the moment we close them at night. It seems all-important, so it often comes as a shock when I tell people that based on my work as a neuropsychologist, this "I" is simply not there—at least not in the way we *think* it is.

On the other hand, this will come as no surprise to those who have studied Eastern religions and philosophical movements, since all of these take as a basic premise the idea that the self as we most commonly think of it does not exist. If this is true, one might then ask, what is left? This question is definitely worth pondering, and we will look at it later after we approach the idea of "no self" through the landscape of scientific findings that point to the unreality of the self and the possible presence of a different model of consciousness.

As I mentioned in the preface, the great success story of neuroscience has been in mapping the brain. We can point to the language center, the face processing center, and the center for understanding the emotions of others. Practically every function of the mind has been mapped to the brain with one important exception: the self. While various neuroscientists have made the claim that the self resides in this or that neural location, there is no real agreement among the scientific community about where to find it—not even whether it might be in the left or the right side of the brain.[1] Perhaps the reason we can't find the self in the brain is because *it isn't there*.

Yet even if we accept as true that there is no self, we cannot deny that there is still a very strong *idea* of self. While neuropsychology has failed to find the seat of the self, it has determined the part of the brain that creates this idea of a self, and we will examine this in detail.

Why does all of this matter? In much the same way I found myself deep in suffering after the loss of my father, each of us will experience plenty of mental pain, misery, and frustration in our lifetimes. Mistaking the voice in our head for a thing and labeling it "me" brings us into conflict with the neuropsychological evidence that shows there is no such thing. This mistake—this illusory sense of self—is the primary cause of our mental suffering. What's more, I contend that it blocks access to the eternal, expansive thread of universal consciousness that is always available to us.

To be clear, mental suffering is different from physical pain. *Pain* occurs in the body and is a physical reaction—like when you stub your toe or break an arm. The *suffering* I speak of occurs in the mind only and describes things such as worry, anger, anxiety, regret, jealousy, shame, and a host of other negative mental states.

I know it's a big claim to say that all of these kinds of suffering are the result of a fictitious sense of self. For now, the essence of this idea is captured brilliantly by Taoist philosopher and author Wei Wu Wei when he writes, "Why are you unhappy? Because 99.9 percent of everything you think, and of everything you do, is for yourself—and there isn't one."[2]

The Structure of This Book

We will start by looking at the brain, its left and right side, and its effects on human cognition and behavior.[3] There are certainly other ways to organize and divide the brain that are important to the process of cognition, such as the hippocampus and the prefrontal cortex mentioned in the preface, but it is my aim to make this topic understandable and enjoyable for everyone. For simplicity's sake, we will mostly talk about the left and right sides of the brain and how they affect our thoughts and behaviors.

First, I will explain the idea that the left brain is an interpreter or story-maker. Pattern recognition, language, mapmaking, and categorization are all located in the left brain, and the evidence suggests that it is exactly these types of functions that collectively lead to the sensation of a self and the strong belief in its absolute truth. We will explore how the unique functions of the left brain give rise not only to the sense of self but also account for why it is so difficult to see beyond this illusion and why this sensation creates so much suffering in the human condition.

Once we understand how the left brain operates, we will take a closer look at the right brain and how it works, which includes things such as finding meaning, our ability to see and understand big-picture ideas, expressing creativity, experiencing emotions, and spatial processing. These are all functions that rely on the right brain. After we have examined both sides of the brain and the processes associated with each, I will speculate on what this information may mean for consciousness and how it could also point beyond the ego illusion and toward the mystery of who we really are.

At the end of each chapter, you will find a section called Explorations. These are exercises or simple thought experiments that provide a chance for a deeper, more hands-on understanding of the concepts discussed. Through these Explorations, I hope you will be able to access the central ideas of this book in novel and exciting ways that go beyond merely thinking about them.

What we discuss here will show that specific studies in neuroscience and psychology strongly suggest what Eastern philosophies have been saying for millennia: namely that this idea of "me" or the "self" that most of us take for granted doesn't exist in the way that we think it does. This may be a new idea for you, and before we begin, I want to make clear that I am not simply trying to convince you that your ego is an illusion by heaping mountains of research on you. Rather, I want to guide you to new experiences and open pathways to using different parts of the brain so that you can determine for yourself whether all this is true or not. Einstein said that a problem cannot be solved with the same level of thinking that created it. In this way, the sense of self created by the left brain cannot be unveiled by hammering away at it with even more thinking from the left brain. My wish is to guide your consciousness to a different way of looking at your experiences and, in so doing, allow you to go beyond the thoughts of the left brain.

I believe this can greatly reduce your mental suffering, as it has mine.

As the ancient Zen axiom states, "No self, no problem."

ONE

Meet the Interpreter— An Accidental Discovery

The brain breathes mind like the lungs breathe air.
—Huston Smith

In the 1960s, Dr. Michael Gazzaniga was a part of a group that performed some of the most interesting and experimental brain surgeries in history. Not only did these experiments reveal how the left and right sides of the brain are responsible for different functions, they also inadvertently laid the groundwork for the idea that the self doesn't exist in the way that we think it does. Gazzaniga himself would be more blunt about the topic later, as he began his 1998 book *The Left-Brain Interpreter*, with a chapter titled "The Fictional Self."

His is a strong indictment of something we take for granted. Considering that the self might be fictional might feel like our distant ancestors first hearing that the Earth was not flat. Both claims seem to defy our very experience. But the idea that the self is fictional is not new—the Buddha said it over 2,500 years ago, and it can be found in the Tao Te Ching, the foundational text of Taoism, also written over two and a half millennia ago, as well as in the writings of certain schools of Hinduism, Advaita Vedanta being one of them.

Is it possible that neuroscience and psychology, through the work of Gazzaniga and others, have now unwittingly proven what these Eastern philosophical traditions stated centuries ago? As we endeavor to answer this question, I will provide you with exercises so that you can experience for yourself whether or not these findings are true. The good news is that—unlike for Gazzaniga's patients—no brain surgery will be required.

Before we move on, it is important to have a basic understanding of how the brain works and the revolutionary findings of Gazzaniga.

To begin, the most interesting aspect of the brain is also one of the most obvious: the brain has two mirror halves connected by a large set of fibers called the corpus callosum. In the 1960s, in research undertaken to try to mitigate severe epilepsy, these 800 million nerve fibers were severed, the central thesis being that seizure activity crossed from one side of the brain to the other over the corpus callosum, increasing the severity of seizures. Doctors Roger Sperry and Michael Gazzaniga believed that by cutting this bridge between the two sides of the brain, seizures would be easier to control. They were correct, and Sperry would win the Nobel Prize in 1981 for this work.

While each side of the brain specializes in certain types of tasks, both sides are usually in continuous communication. When this connection was disrupted, however, it became possible to study the job of each side of the brain in isolation. For example, until this connection was disrupted, scientists relied on either brain damage or indirect methods to test for differences between the left and right brain. However, with the sides disconnected in these epileptic patients, scientists could test each on its own and gain insight into the functional differences between the left and right sides of the brain. These patients were referred to as "split-brain" patients.

To understand this research, it is also important to know that the body is cross-wired: that is, all the input and output from the right half of the body crosses over and is processed by the left brain, and vice versa. This crossover is also true for vision, so that the left half of what we see goes to the right side of the brain, and vice versa. Again, this only became obvious in the split-brain patients. Research with these subjects led to one of the most important discoveries about the left side of the brain—one that has yet to be fully appreciated by modern psychology or the general public.

Gazzaniga determined that the left side of the brain created explanations and reasons to help make sense of what was going on.[1] The left brain acted as an "interpreter" for reality. Furthermore, Gazzaniga found that this interpreter was often completely and totally *wrong*. This finding should have rocked the world, but most people haven't even heard of it. To gain a better understanding of how this split brain works, let's look at some of these studies and their findings in more detail.

The Classic Studies

In one of Gazzaniga's early studies, a split-brain patient had a picture of a chicken's foot presented to the left brain only, and a picture of a snow scene was shown to his right brain only. Then, the patient had several pictures shown to both sides of the brain simultaneously and was asked to pick which one was the most related to the original images they were shown. Each side of the brain performed perfectly; the right brain (using the left hand) pointed to a picture of a snow shovel, whereas the left brain (using the right hand) pointed to a picture of a chicken. Then things got more interesting.

The experimenter asked the patient a simple question: "Why is your left hand pointing to a snow shovel?" Keep in mind, when the experimenter was talking to the split-brain patient, he was talking only to the patient's left brain, since the left brain controls speech. The left brain should have said, "I haven't talked to the right brain in a long time, I don't know why it does what it does with that left hand," but it didn't. Without hesitation, the left brain said, "Oh, that's simple: the chicken foot goes with the chicken and you need a shovel to clean out the chicken coop." The patient stated this with absolute confidence. Here is what's most important about this: the talking left side of the brain easily came up with a plausible and coherent, but *completely incorrect* explanation based on the evidence it had available.

In another example, researchers presented the word *walk* to a patient's right brain only. The patient immediately responded to the request and stood up and started to leave the van in which the testing was taking place. When the patient's left brain (language side) was asked why he got up to walk, again the interpreter came up with a plausible but *completely incorrect* explanation: "I'm going into the house to get a Coke." In another exercise, the word *laugh* was presented to the right brain and the patient complied. When asked why she was laughing, her left brain responded by cracking a joke:

"You guys come up and test us each month. What a way to make a living!" Remember, the correct answer here would have been, "I laughed because you asked me to."

Think about the significance of this for a moment. The left brain was simply making up interpretations, or stories, for events that were happening in a way that made sense to that side of the brain (a shovel is needed for a chicken coop) or as if it had directed the action (I got up because I needed a drink, or I laughed at my own joke). Neither of these explanations was true, but that was unimportant to the interpretive mind, which was convinced that its explanations were the correct ones.

Dr. V. S. Ramachandran, one of the most innovative neuroscientists of the twentieth century, shared a theory of the left brain that is very similar to Gazzaniga's. After conducting his own experiments, Ramachandran found that the left brain's role is one of beliefs and interpretation and that *it had little regard for reality in making up its interpretations.*

For instance, Ramachandran's experiments included subjects whose right brain was severely damaged— leaving the left side of the body paralyzed. With this level of damage to the right brain, the left brain is effectively running the show. When Ramachandran asked one affected subject if she could move her paralyzed left hand, she replied, "Yes. It's not paralyzed." Another one of Ramachandran's subjects claimed that her paralyzed left arm was actually stronger than her right and that she could lift a large table an inch and a half off the ground with it. Others used rationalization as an explanation for the paralysis. They would say things like "I don't want to move my arm, it hurts," or, "The medical students have been prodding me all day and I don't want to move it right now." As in the studies of Gazzaniga, the left brain was simply making up a story about reality without any regard for the truth.

Over the last forty years, several additional studies have shown that the left side of the brain excels at creating an explanation for what's going on, even if it isn't correct. The truth is that your left brain has been interpreting reality for you your whole life, and if you are like most people, you have never understood the full implications of this.

For example, in another classic study, people who think, perceive, and behave in ways considered normal were given a choice of a number of similar items and were asked which they liked the best.[2] Most people are unaware that we have a right-side preference; that is, if you have a number of similar items in front of you, you will have a tendency to prefer the thing on the right. In this study, the researchers noted this tendency. However, when asked, "Why do you like that item?" no one said it was because of a preference for where it was placed. Again, the left brain created a fictitious but plausible theory, and the subjects would say things like, "I just like the color," or, "I just like the texture of that one."

Beyond that, when confronted with the reality— that a right-side preference is natural in most normal human brains—virtually all subjects denied it and disbelieved it. Some even implied that the experimenter was a "madman." Their brain could not handle the idea that they had chosen something not because of what their inner pilot self actually preferred, but due to an arbitrary criterion. This broke through the ego addiction's fog, and for most people this can be a jarring and uncomfortable experience.

Misattributed Arousal

A few more classic studies implicitly suggest that the self is not what it appears to be. Misattributed arousal is the idea that when our nervous system is stimulated or excited—when our blood pressure goes up and our heart beats faster—the left-brain interpreter will make up a story about the origin of this arousal, and often that story is completely wrong. In exactly the same way that the left brain of a split-brain subject creates a theory to explain reality ("you need a shovel for the chicken coop"), these studies have demonstrated that even people who still have intact communication between the two hemispheres create erroneous stories when it comes to unexplained arousal. That is to say that arousal and passion—among other intense emotions—can quickly overcome our ability to reason, leaving our left-brain interpreter free to make up a story that it believes is a solid fit.

In a now famous study,[3] men were instructed to cross over a safe bridge or a scary one. The latter bridge was only 5 feet wide, 450 feet long, and it would sway and wobble in the wind over a steep drop to rocks and shallow rapids. As you can imagine, this second bridge was designed to cause rapid heartbeat and shortness of breath—namely, to simulate arousal. After the male subjects crossed the respective bridges, a female assistant asked them to fill out a questionnaire and make up a short story about a picture they were shown. Finally, the men then had an opportunity to ask the assistant for her phone number in order to call at a future time to "learn more about the experiment." Nine out of eighteen males who crossed the scary bridge called her back, compared to only two out of sixteen males on the less arousing, safer bridge. Their brains had told a story that connected their increased arousal to the female assistant.

You might ask how we know they were actually attracted to the female assistant. We know this because when the researchers analyzed the stories the men had written about the pictures, the scary bridge group's had more sexual themes. This suggests that the interpreter can be rather whimsical in its interpretations and is easily distracted.

Other researchers have explored this same phenomenon by having a female research assistant tell male subjects that they were going to have their balance tested.[4] They were blindfolded and put in a dental chair that would lean back. A loud noise aligned with an "accidental" backward tilt of the chair likely stimulated the nervous systems in the subjects. After the tilting, and compared to control tests, male subjects found the female research assistant more attractive.

In a second study, the female research assistant was replaced with a male. After the arousing incident, male subjects *disliked* the male assistant more than in the control tests. These studies indicate that both attraction and dislike can be just another interpretation of the left brain, and the faster our hearts are beating and the more we are sweating, the more intense that interpretation.

A different pair of researchers asked people to rate the attractiveness of an individual by showing them a photograph—but they were only shown this photograph either before or after they rode a roller coaster.[5] Attractiveness ratings were higher after the subject rode the roller coaster because the interpreter mistook the arousal of the ride as the arousal of attraction. This research has also helped reveal the intelligence and sophistication of the left-brain interpreter. The arousal effect was not present for those riding with a romantic partner! In other words, if you—or rather your left brain—is already in a relationship, no degree of caffeine or amusement park rides will result in finding a stranger more attractive.

In one of Gazzaniga's original studies of the split-brain patients,[6] the experimenters presented the right brain with a video of a person being thrown into a fire. This very likely aroused the patient's nervous system and stimulated fear in the right brain, but the subject's left brain was clueless as to why and left searching for an explanation. She said, "I don't know why, but I feel kind of scared. I feel jumpy. I don't like this room, or maybe you are making me nervous." Later, to another researcher, her left brain said, "I know I like Dr. Gazzaniga, but right now I'm scared of him for some reason."

These studies strongly suggest that we live our lives under the direction of the interpreter, and for most of us the mind is a master we are not even aware of. We may become angry, offended, sexually aroused, happy, or fearful, and we do not question the authenticity of these thoughts and experiences. While it is clear that these experiences are happening to us, we somehow retain the idea that we are still in charge of it all.

Now I would invite you to think about the interpretive mechanism of your own mind in light of what I've just told you about these experiments. For instance, if something noticeable happens, say a person cuts you off in traffic, someone gets up and suddenly runs out of a room, or an attractive person looks at you a second longer than normal, you hear a voice in your head that creates an explanation of the event: "He is a jerk," "They must have forgotten something," or "He or she is interested in me." Notice that those are all interpretations; they may be true or they may not be. However, because many people are not conscious of the left-brain interpreter, they can't even consider that their thoughts are interpretations, but rather feel secure they are seeing things "as they really are."

I'm sure you can remember a time when you interpreted a situation—or even made a problem out of it—only to realize later you'd gotten it wrong. Think about the time you thought a friend was mad at you but found out later they weren't, or you were confident you were going to get that new job but no one ever called. Most of these instances are fairly insignificant and we quickly attribute them to "I made an assumption," but this explanation fails on two counts.

The first is that the interpretive mind is constantly making interpretations without a full account of the facts and it believes these interpretations to be true, much of the time without doubting its conclusion. When an interpretation is later revealed to be not true, the interpretive mind sometimes labels it a mistake, but based on the findings of these early experiments, it's safe to say that many of these interpreted mistakes go unrealized and we never know it. As with the split-brain patient who thought a snow shovel was to clean out a chicken coop or got up to get something to drink, these studies indicate that when actions or facts arise from someplace to which the left brain does not have access, the interpretive portion of our mind will simply explain them. Again, this explanation *may have nothing to do with reality*.

The second thing that is overlooked in the explanation "I made an assumption" is the presumption of "I." In these experiments, the "I" that makes an assumption is really just the interpretive portion of the mind. We have already seen that this "I" can be wrong about so many things in the "outside" world, so is it possible then that the "I" is even wrong about the interpretation of itself? This is what Gazzaniga is getting at when he talks about "Our Fictional Self."

This is also what the spiritual traditions of the East have been saying for over 2,500 years. These traditions, and Buddhism in particular, state unequivocally that the idea of self is a very convincing fiction. Further, they suggest that realizing and accepting that the self is a fiction can lead to the end of suffering.

Why would they make this connection? Well, the inaccurate explanations generated by the left brain, as well as the presupposition of this "me," are the most prevalent causes of internal suffering we experience as humans. Let's look at a simple, real-life example of this.

I have a friend who was convinced that her coworkers didn't like her. She would talk about it daily and become upset. It got so bad that she dreaded going to the office every day. Then something happened at work and she found out that this narrative built around her coworkers was completely false; in fact, the opposite was true. Upon learning this, she gained a very deep insight into how her left brain had interpreted a situation completely inaccurately and she had suffered as a result.

The big difference between the Eastern spiritual traditions and psychology is that the former has recognized this experientially and the latter did so experimentally (and accidentally, for that matter). And this means that those who study and teach psychology are still largely unable to appreciate what it means to experience the interpreter as a fiction.

Perhaps this explains why the world of psychology has paid so little attention to the implications of Gazzaniga's findings. In my own experience having lectured on this topic for twenty years, toward the end of a talk I'm just sure that students will throw things at me, rebel and protest, or simply walk out when I say the evidence suggests the self as we think of it doesn't exist. Yet again and again, the students sit there and continue to take notes after I have completely challenged their ideas of who they think they are. I can ask over and over why they have no reaction to this bombshell I've dropped on them, and yet every time I'm met with blank faces and the occasional nervous laugh in hopes that I'll move on to another topic. When I do get a reaction, it seems similar to what other researchers have had to deal with: that perhaps I am a madman.

As I've said, the self has several built-in mechanisms to ensure it is taken seriously. The importance of these experiments may be easy to ignore cognitively, but understanding and experiencing the profound ramifications of this work can radically change your life. I say this because even though the left-brain interpreter is always on and cannot be turned off, once it is recognized—or that is to say, once we become aware of its constant interpretations—a new awareness of ourselves and the world begins. Instead of being so identified with the "me" in our heads, we find ourselves noticing things like "that's my left-brain interpreter telling stories." When the stories it creates don't evoke as strong a mental or emotional reaction, our suffering lessens as a result.

Exploration

Here's a quick one. Take a ten-second look around and make a mental note of what you see. When you're done, return and continue to read.

What's on your list? I'll bet it includes things like table, chair, tree, grass, car, computer, etc. I will also bet that the word *nothing* is not on your list. That's very interesting, because as we will explore in a later chapter, the vast majority of what is actually out there and connects things in a way that the left brain cannot process is nothing or empty space. This quick exercise is designed to show you how the left side of the brain works: it focuses on objects in space, labels them, categorizes them, and tries to make sense out of them. We have become such experts at organizing our perceptions into categories and patterns that it's difficult to see reality in any other way.

As we move forward, here are some questions to consider: Because the left brain looks outward and only focuses on objects, categorizes them, and labels them, is it possible that it also looks inward and does the same thing? In other words, does the left brain see thought happening in the brain and continuously create a "thing" out of the process of thinking, which it then labels "me"? Is the sense of self related to seeing patterns in randomness? Is it possible that the self we invest so much in is nothing more than a story to help explain our behaviors, the myriad events that go on in our lives, and our experiences in the world?

Have you ever looked up at the stars in the night sky or the clouds during the day and been convinced some pattern was out there? Is it possible that you might be making that same mistake every day when you look within and find an ego or self?

TWO

Language and Categories— The Tools of the Interpreting Mind

*The mind is a tool. The question is,
do you use the tool or does the tool use you?*
—Zen proverb

Now that we have met the left-brain interpreter and demonstrated how it is constantly analyzing our experience and coming up with stories about reality— regardless of whether or not they are true—it is time to introduce you to two of the primary tools the left-brain interpreter uses: language and categorization. Taking a closer look at these two favorite mechanisms of the left brain, we can see how these very tools turned inward are instrumental in the creation of a sense of self.

To begin, I'd like to tell you about the curious case of Louis Victor Leborgne, who mysteriously lost his ability to speak at the age of thirty.[1] While he could still understand speech, the only word he could say was *tan*, which eventually became his nickname. After

Tan's death, physician and scientist Paul Broca discovered damage in the left front part of Tan's brain, the part that is responsible for the overt production of speech—which is now called Broca's area. So even though Tan could understand language and still communicate with others, the part of his brain that controlled speech had been damaged to the point that his ability to speak was restricted to the one word. In Tan's case, the right side of his brain remained unimpaired, so this served as one of the first instances for science to learn which part of the brain was central to speech.

While the right brain does not control speech, we know from Tan's case and the research on the split-brain patients that it understands the written and spoken word. That is how split-brain patients were able to understand written commands shown to the right brain only, like "walk" from the experiments we discussed in the previous chapter. When a word was presented to the left visual field/right brain only (the right visual field was left blank and thus the left brain had no input), the patient's right brain must have been able to read the word or the subject would not have enacted the command. This landmark case, in addition to many studies since then, laid the groundwork for our understanding that the left brain is the dominant center for language.[2]

Importantly, this includes the inner speech we use when we talk to ourselves.[3]

Given that language is controlled by the left brain, it's no coincidence that it is the interpreter's main form of expression. This is most noticeable when we communicate with others, but the interpreter also talks to itself in the form of thoughts. This internal dialogue is happening continually for almost everyone on the planet, and it plays a central role in the creation of the mirage that we call the self.

So that begs the question: What exactly is language? Well one could say that language is just a form of map-making. In the same way that a map represents a place, language creates symbols, or words, that represent something else. For instance, a *chair* is called a chair because that symbol, or word, was agreed upon. Even if we all decided to call it a *lemon* instead, it would still be a good place to sit.

In Iain McGilchrist's masterpiece of a book *The Master and His Emissary: The Divided Brain and the Making of the Western World,*[4] he describes the central role of the left brain as a mapmaker to reality, and language is the pen with which the left brain draws. Language can obviously be extremely helpful in communication with others, but the left brain also becomes so dependent on language that it mistakes the map of reality for reality itself. There is an old Zen proverb that points to this problem, advising against "confusing the menu with the food."

When the mind mistakes the map for reality, the result is that we carry on blindly in a world of language-based stories created by the left-brain interpreter. Keeping in mind that the left brain creates stories it believes completely—often without regard to the truth—one could compare this to following an inaccurate map. Anyone who has allowed their smartphone's GPS system to take them down a dead-end road knows how frustrating this can be.

To be clear, there is nothing wrong with making maps in general—we need them. The issue, as scholar Alfred Korzybski, the developer of the field of general semantics, might have speculated, is that the left brain mistakes the map for the territory.[5] We will spend a good deal of time navigating within the framework of this mistake. Our association of our true self with the constant voice in our head is an instance of mistaking the map (the voice) for the territory (who we really are). This error is one of the biggest reasons the illusion of self is so difficult to see.

In what is likely the most studied experiment in the history of psychology, the Stroop effect[6] demonstrates how the left brain takes language literally and mistakes the symbol for the thing itself.

For instance, imagine if you were presented with some basic color swatches and asked to identify the hues you were being shown. This would be easy. Next, imagine that a particular color was presented in the form of a word, say *RED* written in the color red. Your left brain would like this very much. But what would happen if the word were *YELLOW*, but written in the color blue? Your response time to identify the colors correctly will be significantly slower when the word and the color do not match—so much slower that it will be noticeable even without a stopwatch or other instrumentation. This slowed reaction time is what is known as the Stroop effect.

Why does a mere shake-up in symbols and colors cause us to stutter and stall out so badly? Because the left brain confuses the map with the territory, it reads the word *YELLOW* and calls up the actual color yellow instead of the blue it was written in.[7] When the two don't match, reaction time slows down as the brain tries to sort out its confusion. This doesn't happen if you can't read or if the word is in a language that you don't know. I gave this test to both of my kids growing up and noticed that as their left brains began to take the symbols of language more seriously, the Stroop effect slowly increased.

This study points to the immense power that words have on the left side of the brain. It reminds me of what we are often told as children, namely that "sticks and stones will break your bones but words will never hurt you." As it turns out, depending on how seriously we take the processing of the left brain, this could be a lie. Researcher Martin Teicher has found that verbal abuse is at least as harmful as physical abuse and a strong risk factor for depression and other psychological disorders.[8] In modern society, we often take words as seriously as the physical world they represent.

Furthermore, our left brain is so tied to the power of words that it is hard to see their effect. Think of an example in your own life when someone said something to you that you found hurtful. You may have suffered greatly, but the truth is that this person was simply sharing an opinion and expressing it via sounds emanating from their voice box. How is it possible that such a thing "hurt" you? Obviously you were hurt by your interpretation of it or the map that these sounds created in your left brain. Next, imagine for a moment if there were no self to hurt? Would words directed at this "you" ever be seen as a problem?

Another thing to notice about maps is that they necessarily leave out all sorts of details. Of course, this is why real maps are useful. It is much easier to carry a map of the park in your back pocket than the actual park itself. Maps leave out details which could be confusing if you were trying to navigate by every bird, plant, or car on the street.

However, maps stop being useful when they are mistaken for what they represent. You can't play ball in a paper map of a park. In this way, language is an excellent servant but a terrible master. Or put another way, words are wonderful tools, but as the old Zen proverb queries, "Do you use the tool or does the tool use you?"

In my opinion, when you mistake the voice in your head for who you really are, the tool is using you. Language creates a story, and this story—combined with our memories and the sense of a command center behind our forehead—creates an illusion of self that virtually everyone on the planet identifies with. In the same way that we mistake words for what they represent, we also use our linguistics-based thoughts as the basis for a fictional self as a genuine self. Most people are familiar with Helen Keller, who lost both sight and hearing very early in life. It is particularly telling that she states that she only developed a sense of self *after* she learned language.[9]

Let's look at some other ways language can influence our perception of reality. For instance, it is common to label frozen foods "fresh frozen." Such a phrase was the source of one of famed chef Gordon Ramsay's notorious rants. As he so emphatically put it, "fresh frozen . . . there's no such thing: it is either fresh or it is frozen." But marketers know that writing the word *fresh* on the package will change our perception of the food. It is easy to be fooled by what words tell us, because we have put so much stock into language as a reliable map of reality.

In another example, the work of psychologist Elizabeth Loftus has shown that if a group sees the same fender bender and is later divided, the two perceptions of the accident can be altered by words.[10] If one group is asked, "How fast were the cars going when they *smashed* together?" they will report faster speeds than the group asked, "How fast were the cars going when they *bumped* each other?" Simply using the words *smashed* or *bumped* creates two different perceptions of the same reality.

The root of the problem is that many of us do not see language as a representation of reality, but confuse it with reality itself. This mistake contributes significantly to suffering when we take words too seriously. We might be disappointed by frozen food we thought would taste fresh. Taken to a much more significant extreme, we can observe this as a contributing factor in the modern phenomenon of teen suicides that result from online bullying.

A Categorization Expert

Another characteristic of the left brain is its constant propensity to create categories. In fact, almost everything the left brain does, from language to its perception of objects in space, is categorical in nature.

What do we mean by *category*? Categories are just another type of map of reality. They are mental representations that don't exist "out there" in the world, but rather they are only in the human mind—the left side of the brain to be specific. Categories are based on the left brain's ability to see differences and create opposites and are formed when things in the world that are continuous are grouped by some common feature and then treated as one unit.

In terms of human symbolic thought, categories are very useful. If your house were on fire, what would you save? The kids, the dogs, and with time, some jewelry. Suddenly, things that look very different get grouped and treated as one thing: all of the kids (not just Jeremy), all of the dogs (not just the border collie), all of the jewelry (not just the clip-on earrings). To a biologist the category of *mammal* is useful even if it treats dogs and whales as equals. In order to establish these "equivalence classes," other differences must be ignored. This is similar to our last topic of mapmaking because just like mapmaking, categories ignore certain details. Furthermore, categorization intrinsically falls apart in places. Think about black and white and the endless shades of gray between. When does black turn into white? In forming a category, one takes several things and believes that they are one thing, different and separate from everything else. Of course, it's all subjective.

As long as we remember that categories are mental representations (thoughts) only, they can be very useful; in other words, categories exist as "things" only in the mind and only in the act of perceiving them. Issues arise when we believe these "things" are real.

For instance, imagine if you showed up at the university where I teach and asked me to show you the university. After being shown one building after another, you begin to get frustrated and say, "Yes, I've seen this building and that building but where is *the university*?" I would have to point to the left side of my head and say, "it is only up here," because it exists as a category and so it may change depending on whom you talk to. When no one is thinking about it, it doesn't exist at all. The same can be said for countries. Where is the country of Canada when no one is there to perceive it? Of course, I'm not saying the land or buildings disappear, but their division into categories depends on an observer and a judgment. The country of Canada is based upon arbitrary lines on a map—even though we have built a complex system of border crossings. If no one thought of a place called Canada, would it still exist?

Turning inward for a moment, let's consider how this categorization mechanism might be employed by the left brain to create a sense of self. For instance, think of all the ways in which you can answer the question "who are you?" Most people in my shoes would say things like, "I am a man, a father, a husband, a professor, an author," etc. But if you really look, while all of these things point to ways in which I can categorize myself, they don't actually answer the question, "who am I?" Is that because the "I" that I am looking for is more akin to the university or the country of Canada? Sure, the physical entity of my body and my brain is there, but the "I" attached to it only exists as a thought—and only when I think it. Is it possible that you can't definitively answer this question because the "I" you are addressing isn't a thing?

Seen in this light, "I" is simply a useful, categorical fiction, expressed through language. But unlike the categorical fictions of the university or Canada, believing wholeheartedly in the fiction of self—in effect, making the left-brain interpreter the master instead of the servant—has unintended consequences—suffering being one of them.

Furthermore, the left brain's obsession with categories also provides a nice example of how the left brain can tie itself in knots. Which came first, the chicken or the egg? If God created everything, who created God? The deeper you go, the more you are tied up in a causality dilemma with infinite regress.

This is the conundrum of the left brain: there is a limit to its understanding through categorizing and interpreting, and although we can hit that limit quickly and easily, many people, including some of the most well-known psychologists and Western philosophers, disregard this fact and put all their stock in the power of thinking.

To begin to go beyond the interpreter, it's as if one must completely circumvent the question of "How do I think beyond categories?" If someone tried to show you how to not think in categories, this would just be more categories. It might be funny to title a book *How to Not Think Categorically*—which would be one end of just another categorical distinction: that is, categorical vs. noncategorical thinking. *To think is to think in categories, and there is no way around this.* There are, however, other forms of intelligence associated with the right side of the brain that are beyond the capacity of the interpretive mind, and we will look at these a little later.

Judgments

Categories are created by taking something continuous and drawing the proverbial line in the sand to separate one into two. The placement of this line requires a judgment. Without judgment, categories could not exist. In fact, one could go so far as to say the next closest word for *interpreter* would be *judge* (but without the moral aspect of judgment). To interpret is to judge things, and there is no way around this.

Exactly where along the continuum of temperature does cold become hot? When do you get offended? When does good become evil? When does something become a catastrophe? A failure? When does being poor become being rich? When does happiness become sadness? Where do you draw the line for any and all of these?

Recognizing this has immense practical benefits. Simply becoming aware of the interpreter and the endless categories it creates through judgment frees you from being tied to the inevitability of these judgments. That is to say, when you become conscious of the interpreter, you are free to choose to no longer take its interpretations so seriously. In other words, when you realize that everyone's brain is constantly interpreting, in ways that are subjective and often inaccurate or completely incorrect, you might find yourself able to grasp this as "just my opinion" or "the way I see it" rather than "this is the way it is." You begin to see your judgments as simply a different line in the sand than others. When someone approaches you with a "this is the way it is" attitude, you can appreciate that this person is dominated by the left brain, that they are a servant to its master. As a result, there is no need to take their actions or attitudes personally; it's a biological function that they have not yet recognized. This small perspective shift is enough to change how we live with each other and ourselves.

Furthermore, when you become aware that the left brain is just doing its thing, interpreting and judging, the stories it creates don't tend to provoke the physical reaction in your nervous system they once did. A momentary judgment of "They don't like me" doesn't have to spiral into the sweaty palms and increasing heart rate of a mini panic attack. This awareness of the interpreter can profoundly change how you experience the world. In addition, when you begin to observe the interpreter, you find that you make fewer judgments and can take your judgments less seriously. You know that they just happen.

Beliefs

The left-brain interpreter also creates and sustains a collection of categorical thoughts based on judgments and groups them together as likes and dislikes, ideas of right and wrong, and mental models of how things are supposed to be. We collectively call these judgments *our belief system.*

But belief systems are like the university where I teach or the country of Canada: they don't exist "out there" in the world, but only in the left brain and only when people are thinking about them. Take some of the most popular beliefs: my country is the best; my religion is the only true one; I think so-and-so should be president of the country. None of these beliefs exists independently in the world, but only in the mind and only at the moment someone creates them through the process of thinking.

Furthermore, if everyone believes something different, then we cannot all be right. What are the odds that you alone have the right beliefs and everyone else is wrong? When you are heavily identified with your left-brain interpreter where your beliefs are housed, it can seem as if they are no longer a constructed perspective created by thinking, but simply "the way things are."

Beliefs are very interesting, because they do hold very real power over us in some fascinating ways. In fact, science uses and controls for this tool, a subject that most of us are aware of as the placebo effect.[11]

A *placebo* is a procedure or pill that does not do anything. For instance, a placebo might be a saline drip or a sugar pill rather than medication. The placebo effect occurs when a subject is given a placebo, but believes that they are taking the real medication.

Because the brain believes that it is receiving medication for a condition, the subject feels the "effects" of having taken medication, even though nothing with an active ingredient has been administered.[12]

While the mechanisms of the placebo effect are still unknown, somehow the belief that one is taking a pill to help with a particular disease changes the brain in the same way that the treatment drug changes it, as witnessed in certain studies on the placebo effect and Parkinson's patients.[13] As you can surmise, the placebo effect is one of the most powerful examples of the brain making the map/territory error. This is why many experiments are what we call "blind" and the subject does not know whether they are getting the real drug or not. You can't tell a subject, "You are only taking a sugar pill, but I want you to believe it is a real, active drug," or conversely, "You are getting a real drug but I want you to believe it is only a sugar pill." If the brain had this information, it would be impossible for it to accurately "believe" or "act like" the opposite was true, no matter how much we might try. The idea that we cannot control our beliefs is so fundamental to science that a placebo or control group (a group that is monitored and observed as part of an experiment, but upon which no experimental procedures are taken) is actually part of the definition of what constitutes an experiment.

One of the tenets of Eastern philosophy and Buddhism in particular is that we are not our thoughts and beliefs. Of course, when we identify as the interpreter—when we are unaware of its effects and are possessed by it—perhaps then we could say that we *are* in fact our thoughts and beliefs. This is particularly true because some of our beliefs we simply can't change, even if we wanted to. Likes, dislikes, preferences, etc., are all examples of beliefs we have little say in. For instance, can you believe you don't like chocolate if you really do? Could you believe that you are Albert Einstein if I gave you a million dollars? I don't mean simply faking it; could you truly change your central beliefs to be the opposite of what they currently are? Regardless of your efforts, you would not be able to will a belief into existence.

Having no control over beliefs can be a source of anxiety in belief-based religious systems. Many of these systems are set up such that eternal salvation or morality rest upon relying on a certain belief. And since it is impossible to control our beliefs, it may be impossible to be saved, making this a bit nerve-racking. Worse yet, if you believe there is an omnipotent being that can read all your thoughts, you can't simply pretend or make something up like I do when my wife asks me which curtains I like and I pick one.

Let's look at how being overly identified with a belief system can cause suffering. What is the major source of conflict between people? Why do we fight each other? Turn on any news channel and you can confirm the intense suffering that occurs due to opposing belief systems. People die and kill for beliefs all the time, but not just any beliefs—only the ones they believe in without recognizing that they are only beliefs. This is how the interpreter confuses actual reality with a thought-based belief, and it is simply another example of the map/territory mistake. The left-brain interpreter not only creates and maintains these assumptions of the world, but makes them feel as though they are truly how the world really is. This is very unsettling when you consider the left brain's ability to make up stories that have absolutely nothing to do with reality, as case studies have shown.

To be clear, there is nothing wrong with a belief if you see it for what it is: the outcome of a process that goes on in the left brain maintained by a group of brain cells and neurochemistry. The old Zen saying of "Right and wrong are the sickness of the mind" points to this dilemma precisely, as "right" and "wrong" are only beliefs that become a sickness when we take them so seriously they become "the way things are."

Only when we begin to see that the interpreter is creating and maintaining our beliefs can we become less attached to the idea that our own beliefs are "right." This opens us to new ideas and the possibility that for other interpretive minds, it is our beliefs that could be "wrong."

Turning inward for a moment, let's look again at the central question of this book. Is it too much to imagine that the left brain uses all the aforementioned tools of language, categorization, and judgment to create the belief of an individual self? If so, are we so tied to that belief that—in the same way we do with other beliefs—we simply see it as "the way things are," rather than simply another belief?

Holding this possibility in our minds, we can see that once the belief in the individual self is anchored, we then further divide and categorize this individual self and turn this imaginary self into a project for self-improvement. This results in the twin beliefs that "this is how I am," and "this is how I want to be," but this internal split is just more of the left brain doing its job to separate all things into opposing categories.

Even as it is separating and categorizing the entire outer world, the interpreter also works to separate and categorize the inner world into the conflicting beliefs of a controller (present self) and something else to be controlled (future self), creating an inner conflict that cannot be resolved. We are the only species that we know of that can believe in ourselves, lie to ourselves, convince ourselves, love or hate ourselves, accept ourselves, push and even pull ourselves. These beliefs are fundamental to the human story, as much a part of the dramas relayed by the ancient Greek poet Homer as they are playing out in the daily headlines today.

Explorations

Let's try a few hands-on explorations to bring to light some of the ways that the left-brain interpreter operates.

Notice the Power of Yes vs. No

This exercise is similar to the Stroop effect and based on research into how the brain responds to seeing the words *no* and *yes*.[14] For instance, say that you encountered a billboard that simply read **NO** in bold letters. Your brain would likely have a reaction to seeing **NO** written out. On the other hand, consider if you saw a billboard that said **YES**. Your brain would likely also have a reaction to that.

While some parts of the reaction might be the same—surprise, curiosity, etc.—they would not be the same reaction. **NO** makes you feel a certain way, as does **YES**. Place your hands to isolate on the page the word *no* as illustrated here and read it internally for a few moments. Do the same thing with the word *yes*. Do you notice any difference within yourself? Does *yes* have a positive feeling for you while *no* the other? This points to the power we give words.

NO   YES

Finally, consider one last billboard. This one is written in Chinese or Russian or French or another language that you can't read. Whether the billboard says yes or no in this foreign language is irrelevant—because you are unlikely to have had a brain reaction at all to a form of written language that you can't understand. You can likely notice in yourself the internal responses you have to the words *no* and *yes* when they are presented without any further context. Observing this subtle effect on you demonstrates the emotional, mental, and even physical connection we have to certain words.

Spotting Your Beliefs

Can you spot your beliefs? Take something such as a political preference. Maybe you believe that Democrats could run a country much better than Republicans or vice versa. Do you see this as a belief or do you believe it? I invite you to spend a few minutes and really think about the merits of the opposite position of one of your most cherished beliefs, as this is a good way to see it for what it is: a thought that exists in your left brain only. Doing this with more of your beliefs can lessen your identification with the left-brain interpreter.

The Power of Paradox

Before we move on, let's take a quick look at the power of paradox, as it often trips up the interpreter and for this reason paradox is a turnoff to those deeply possessed or controlled by the left brain. Paradox is also more attractive to those less identified with the interpreter. Notice how consciousness changes when confronted with the following inconsistencies:

"The next sentence is true.
The previous sentence is false."

Here is another nice example that might take a little longer:

"This sentense containes three errors."

There are two spelling errors but then there is also the error that there are only two errors, which makes three, so there really isn't a third error. It can only be right if it is wrong, which blurs the right-wrong distinction.

Finally, consider this:

> "Whoever wrote the last two
> examples doesn't know how to write."

See the conundrum?

Perhaps these paradoxes are just modern forms of the much older practice of Zen Buddhism: the use of koans to trip up or stop the interpreting mind from its constant thinking.[15] Paradoxes like "What did you look like before you were born?" or "What is the sound of one hand clapping?" sound silly from the perspective of the interpretive mind, since they cannot be answered categorically.

THREE

Pattern Perception and the Missing Self

*Identity is merely a pattern of events
in time and space. Change the pattern
and you have changed the person.*
—Nisargadatta Maharaj

In the last chapter we looked at a few of the tools of the interpreter: language, categorization, beliefs, and judgment. The left brain uses these tools in such a way that we could say it is really something of a pattern-making machine. In fact, I would argue that it is the most advanced pattern-perception machine in the cosmos.

To illustrate this, consider what language and categorization have in common: both of these functions are dependent upon one's ability to find and determine patterns. For instance, in language, you have to determine the pattern of subject-verb agreement, the patterns that dictate grammar and verb conjugation. For categorization, it's the pattern that determines what is or isn't part of a group. Remember, the only difference between being "confused" and being "coufnsed," is the categorical arrangement of the letters. If the left brain excels at both of these things—then it supports the idea that the left brain is the seat of pattern recognition.[1]

Just like categories and beliefs, most of us have completely forgotten that patterns only exist in the mind and not out in reality. Furthermore, our ability to see patterns is so intrinsic to how we experience and interact with the world that we don't even notice all the ways in which our pattern-perceiving left brain is doing its thing.

For instance, the activity you are engaged in right now—reading—would not be possible without your ability to recognize patterns. Reading involves seeing a series of straight lines, curved lines, and dots on paper and making sense out of them in a way that is incredibly powerful and unique. We take our ability to do this for granted to the point that we forget that all we are seeing is marks on paper. We "remember" this when we see something written in a language we don't understand, if only partially, as the mind recognizes even this as "a language I don't understand." We see the pattern and categorize it as "foreign language."

While we are on the topic of reading, let's consider two related specialties of the left brain: grammar and spelling.[2] Both are patterns and both have rules, and patients with damage to the left brain have difficulties with both, primarily because both are about recognizing "correct" or "incorrect" patterns.

When it comes to grammar, 76 percent of the world's languages are structured as either subject, object, verb ("Jim the apple ate") or subject, verb, object ("Jim ate the apple"). Maybe it was not a coincidence that Yoda from *Star Wars*, with his Eastern philosophy overtones, always used an object, subject, verb structure (e.g., "Much to learn, you still have."). English-speaking left brains are not accustomed to this structure, and one wonders if this was an attempt, conscious or otherwise, to sidestep the rule-based interpreter. After all, in the end Luke's lesson was to trust his gut over his interpretive mind in order to become a Jedi.

Spelling also relies on our ability to see patterns. What is the difference between *sing* and *sign* other than the organization of the letters? I have great difficulty with these two words and often email my students that I will *sing* them up for my classes. This symptom of dyslexia is likely related to the left brain. Research has shown that in dyslexics across many world languages, the left hemisphere is both smaller (compared to non-dyslexic controls) and also has areas that vary from the "norm."[3]

Other modes of visual expression are completely dependent on our ability to recognize patterns. Take a look at the next image.

Many of you will see the actor Brad Pitt here. However, let's be clear that this image *is only ink dots on paper*, and seeing that pattern as a representation of the person we refer to as Brad Pitt occurs only in the mind. Here again, the implications that arise from our left brain's ability to see a pattern in this series of ink dots are quite fascinating.

We can all agree that this image isn't the "real" Brad Pitt, but rather an illusionary representation of him. When we think again of the major question of this book, is it possible that the left brain looks within and sees an illusionary representation called the self? The big difference, of course, is that unlike this drawing of Brad Pitt, almost everyone believes that the self is real.

Psychology's first formal recognition of the pattern-perceiving part of the brain was likely due to the work of Dr. Hermann Rorschach, who created the famous inkblot test back in the 1920s.[4] In a Rorschach test, a subject is presented with an inkblot and asked to take a look and say what they see in the image. You can try this for yourself now. Take a look at the image on the next page and respond with what images you can see in it.

This is called a *projective test* because it was believed at the time of its creation that patients would project any inner or unconscious issues on the random inkblot, but what Rorschach had really discovered was that the

pattern perceiver could *always* make sense of randomness and see something. (The main issue with this test is that while a patient may expose certain tendencies of their pattern perceiver, this is only processed by yet another pattern perceiver in the therapist.)

While seeing patterns that aren't there as in the Rorschach test can seem innocuous, upon closer inspection it may provide us with a hint of how the left brain created our sense of self—by seeing a pattern that isn't there. In other words, perhaps our pattern-perceiving machine looks within and finds a single point of perception, remembers a series of likes and dislikes, judgments, beliefs, etc., and creates the pattern of "me."

Identifying patterns is a helpful and necessary tool to navigate the world in many ways, but it is also true that by constantly looking for patterns the left brain "complicates" what is perceived in a way that can be unnecessary and unhelpful. For instance, one study involved a simple test where viewers guessed whether a light was going to appear on the top or bottom of a computer screen. Unbeknownst to the subjects, in the test the image randomly appeared on the top 80 percent of the time. Most everyone quickly deduced that it appeared on the top more often, but because the left brain is constantly looking to "solve the puzzle," it tried to find a solid pattern in the random occurrences. As a result, the subjects only guessed correctly about 68 percent of the time. That number may still sound impressive, but when the test was repeated with rats, which lack our complicated pattern-seeking interpreter, the rats always picked the top, so they guessed correctly 80 percent of the time.[5] *This is a perfect example of the interpreter spending time trying to find a pattern for a story that doesn't exist.* So in this case, the left brain "lost" when compared to rats, and most interestingly, none of the participants had the slightest clue that they were creating patterns that were not there.

By seeing patterns that are not there, the mind creates stories that aren't true, and as we've previously discussed, this can lead to unnecessary suffering, anxiety, and depression. Let's return to the example of my friend who thought she was having trouble at work with her coworkers. She witnessed them huddled in the corner whispering to one another, and her left brain surmised a pattern, namely that they were plotting against her. She experienced a wave of sadness, fear, anxiety, and so on, and spent a good amount of time agonizing over it. Later she found out they were planning a surprise birthday party for her instead. While this example may seem trivial, I invite you to notice how your own left brain sees patterns that later turn out to not be there, which is the same as creating mental stories about events that just aren't true.

There is also some evidence that neurotransmitters affect our pattern-perception capability. Because of this, it is important to note that the two sides of the brain differ in terms of their neurochemistry.[6] The left brain is dominant for dopamine, whereas the right brain is dominant for serotonin and norepinephrine. There are many functions associated with dopamine that range from the euphoria of falling in love to the movements of the body. Since the 1950s, it has also been thought that schizophrenia is the result of too much dopamine. One of the hallmarks of schizophrenia is seeing patterns that are not there, that is to say hallucinations.

One fascinating study found that subjects who had an increased amount of dopamine were more likely to find patterns.[7] The study used two groups of subjects:

one group was comprised of people with a propensity to see patterns in random images (the believers), and the other was made up of people who looked at the same random images and almost never saw patterns (the skeptics). In the experiment, the two groups were shown images from which they had to detect if they were being shown a real word or face or a scrambled word or face. Both groups made mistakes: the believers saw patterns when there were none, and the skeptics often missed when a real face or word was on the screen. When dopamine was increased in both groups, the skeptics started to make the mistake of seeing patterns when there were none. Dopamine turned up the perception of patterns even when no patterns were present. When the dopamine wore off, the skeptics' left brain went back to normal as did their responses.

Another interesting thing uncovered in pattern-perception research is how a participant's tendency to see patterns increased when the researchers threatened the participant's sense of self.[8] In one such study, researchers presented participants with a picture made up simply of visual noise (random variations of brightness and colors) either at a time when they felt safe or right before they jumped out of a plane.[9] The act of jumping out of a plane presents an acute fear that the pattern known as the self may soon come to an end.

Those about to jump were more likely to believe that they saw a pattern in the randomness (numbers imbedded in the random noise) versus the control group.

The tendency of the self to defend its own image through more thinking is a hallmark of understanding in Buddhism. Experienced meditators describe how in meditation, as the mind begins to still and the voice in the head speaks less frequently, there is often a rush of thoughts that are most important to sustaining the self-image. This is how meditators can notice what mental stories and thought patterns are their most prevalent preoccupations, as the mind reverts to replaying these topics as a defense against slowing down. Some Eastern teachers explain that the mind "keeps talking" in this way because it's the only way it can exist. This is consistent with my view that the self is more like a verb than a noun. It only exists when we think it does, because the process of thinking creates it.

The combination of these studies in neuropsychology and Buddhist teaching suggests that when the pattern of the self feels threatened or exposed, thinking shifts in a way to support a new or reinterpreted version of itself. You can quickly examine this idea for yourself. For instance, have you ever felt a threat to your ego? Ever felt stupid or embarrassed? In those moments your sense of self wasn't as secure as you thought it was, so you likely shifted and reinterpreted the events to account for this unexpected change. This reinterpreting or reinvesting can happen in a variety of ways. You may do anything from discounting others (i.e., "their opinion is of no value") to refocusing your identity another way ("well, I may not be as rich as they are, but I am much smarter!" or focus on how patriotic you are, or how spiritual, or any other prized pattern of the self that compensates for the area in which your ego felt threatened). From a neuropsychological perspective, we could say that all of these defenses are caused by the left brain's mechanism readjusting to unexpected pattern changes. From a Buddhist perspective, we could say that the self is recreating itself in response to the threat of dissolution. In my view, they are one and the same.

In 2006, Doctors Travis Proulx and Steven Heine reviewed research across various disciplines to describe exactly what happens when a belief is threatened.[10] What they concluded was that when this occurs, humans turn to other beliefs and increase their intensity. As they put it, "When committed beliefs are violated, people experience an arousal state that prompts them to affirm other beliefs to which they are committed." The authors reported that study after study had the same finding. When the reality of one pattern is challenged, subjects would increase their belief in some other pattern to compensate. That is, when the belief in the safety and security of the self was challenged, another form of self-identity increases.

I experienced this myself recently when I attended a gathering of about eighty faculty members at my university. I wasn't sure of the purpose of the gathering and didn't pay much attention to the opening remarks. Without thinking, I stood up and introduced myself to those around me. After only three seconds I realized that no one was introducing themselves and that I was stuck in a rather absurd moment. As I sat down, my interpreter "lost it." The voice in my head kept trying to redirect to other familiar patterns in my life (such as family or friends) in order to minimize this existential anxiety and to keep me from thinking too hard about what it perceived as a threat to my "self" or "self-worth," aka embarrassment.

There are other times in ordinary life that the pattern perceiver runs across an unexplainable anomaly in our behavior or our doing something we may describe as "out of character," but figuring out why could take too much time and effort to work into the grand pattern of self. In these instances, the left brain may simply dismiss them as times in which we are "not ourselves" or something has "come over us." Most often, we simply leave these anomalies a mystery, soon forgotten as the single grand pattern comes back online.

The point of all of this is to make clear to you that sitting upon your shoulders is the most advanced pattern-perception machine in the known universe and that it goes almost completely unappreciated. Even computers with the most advanced AI cannot match the pattern perception of the average human. We are seeing patterns, categorizing things, even creating a language to describe these patterns—all at lightning speed.

Now, consider again what happens when such a powerful pattern-perception machine turns inward. Was there ever a chance it *wouldn't* "find" a self, an ego, a consistent something, out of the thoughts and mental reactions that occur in your brain? Is it possible that the missing self—the one that neuropsychology can't find and the Buddha says doesn't exist—is a mirage created by the very mechanisms of the brain itself? An interesting experiment to find out might be to give AI all of the qualities of the left brain and then turn it loose. I believe that eventually it too would look within and believe that it has a self.

Lastly, I want to add that this pattern-perception machine in the left brain is a biological function that is working all the time and virtually impossible to stop. That being said, simply by becoming aware of the left brain's propensity to see patterns, we can begin to take them less seriously. This has significant benefits for how we experience the world, including reducing our suffering.

The Missing Self

As a way to bring together everything we've covered so far, I'd like you to consider the next image. Remember the specialties of the left brain: to tell a story, to create an explanation, to categorize, to see patterns even if there isn't one to see. In the image, consider the dark circles and bent lines as representing the various parameters of the self, and at the center is the story that pulls it all together. This story is represented by the triangle in the center of the image.

As you have noticed by now, there is no actual triangle in the image. Seeing it is a function of interpreting the inverse of the lines and circles which surround it. In my view, seeing this triangle is like looking at your own individual self, because both are created in the same way: by inference.

The same left-brain process that allows you to see the categorical boundaries of the circles and lines and surmise the image of the triangle has also looked within, used the same processes, and surmised that there is an individual self. Both the triangle and the inner self are strongly suggested by the surrounding information, but upon closer inspection one can see that they are only suggested and have no real physical existence.

This is consistent with what Buddhism, Taoism, and other schools of Eastern thought have been saying for thousands of years: the self we think of as "me" is an illusion, an inference. Based on what I have presented so far, I hope you can see that several studies in neuropsychology are now suggesting the same thing. To be clear, saying the self is an illusion doesn't mean that it doesn't exist at all, but rather that it's akin to a mirage in the middle of the desert. The vision of the oasis is real, but the oasis itself isn't. In this same way, the image of the self is real, but when we look at the image, we find it is simply that, an image and nothing more. The image of both, the oasis and the self, is really just another idea or thought and only there the moment it is being thought of.

The left brain has created this illusion of self by noticing a pattern of categorical differences between you and others and combining those observations with memory, preferences, and the perspective of the "pilot," who seems to be steering the ship of the brain and body. Our definition of self depends in part on our difference from others. There is no "me" without "not me."

This is fairly easy to see in your own life. You categorize and define your "self" in relation to others. For me, I use descriptors like father, professor, author, etc., to distinguish "me" from everyone around me. How do you do it? If you feel you are funny and intelligent, that judgment places you in social categories that depend upon other people being boorish and not so smart. Otherwise your categories would have no meaning. If you are an extrovert, you need introverts for a comparison. If you are male, you need female in the same way we see in the classic reversible symbol of Taoism: yang needs yin to define what it is.

Psychology and many self-help practices play the game of categories regularly, when we say things like "this is how I am, and this is how I want to be." We create an image of ourselves, split that image, and then suffer when one imaginary image can't live up to that "better" imaginary image. We want to be smarter, more attractive, more successful, etc., and all of these ideas are our "problems." The great tragedy here is that we never realize that none of these conditions will ever be met completely to the satisfaction of the self because the self must continue to think in order to stay in existence and therefore will always change the measuring stick— always adding a new "better" to fall short of.

As a reminder, when I say we suffer, in this context I mean we generate thoughts and feelings of sadness, disappointment, grief, what have you, as we reject one imaginary version of ourselves in favor of another. This is simply the left brain doing its thing and nothing more. When we identify entirely with the left brain and believe that it's us, however, the suffering can be overwhelming.

One more caveat. You might be feeling guilty or beating yourself up in this moment for not recognizing that the interpreter is a transparent image. This won't help in overcoming suffering one bit, since this process of self-flagellation is exactly how the interpreter continues to create itself. It is just more of the "this is how I am" and "this is how I want to be" game that simply produces more problems for the interpreter to think about. Remember, *to think is to think categorically, and there is no way around this.* The trick is to become less identified with your thoughts, to not take them so seriously, to see them as "happenings" rather than "the way things really are."

As a last example, take a look at the below image. Where did the triangle go?

While the inference of the triangle is gone, the space that made up the triangle did not actually go anywhere; it was always pure emptiness and it still is. Perhaps this is why one of the core tenets of Eastern philosophies is emptiness and the notion that everything that exists arises from this emptiness. What allows us to notice this emptiness at all? Perhaps it is something we could call awareness or consciousness (something we will talk more about in a later chapter): simply the observance that the space is there. That's really all that can be said about it, and of course the left brain hates this, because as a lover of language, categories, and maps, it has reached the end of its ability to use its tools.

In my view, believing that the left-brain interpreter is "you" is akin to looking at the night sky and believing the constellation Orion is really out there as an entity, rather than a group of stars seen from a particular angle, which the mind has made into a pattern and labeled. While it may initially sound a little depressing to know that nothing is real in the way we might think it is, you may find a sense of relief in this—like putting down a heavy sack you've been taught to carry your whole life.

Another way to think of the fictional self or ego is that its addiction to interpreting works like a drug. Every day it needs to get its fix, and it does that in a variety of ways: telling stories about what it perceives, comparing and categorizing itself against others, judging things as right or wrong—and it uses all of these processes to define "you" as "yourself."

As you can see by now, a vast array of problems can come out of this thinking. Rather than embrace reality as it is, the left brain is hopelessly addicted to storytelling and interpretations about reality, which provide a short-term hit of purpose and meaning but an inevitable crash of suffering. And most people never even know this cycle is going on.

Some may reject this idea for its simplicity. How can so much of human suffering and problems come down to something as simple as blaming an out-of-control left brain? As an academic, I hear this objection to simplicity often, and I can't help but see in it the voice of the left brain, which is drawn toward complex abstractions and therefore suspects simple truth. In this vein, I wonder if one day when someone finally presents a Theory of Everything that connects and explains all known forces in the universe, it might appear too simple to be believed.

So far, we've examined how the left brain functions and illustrated how much of the suffering we experience as humans may be linked to an unbalanced left brain creating an illusionary sense of self and proclaiming that this illusion is the true master. In the next few chapters we will focus on the right brain, and how the left-brain interpreter has dismissed, devalued, or downplayed it—all, in my view, to our detriment as a species. The good news is that as you bring your awareness to the functions of the right brain, you come into a state of balance and experience less suffering as a result.

Exploration
How Many Yous in a Day?

The left brain is seduced by consistency, even though the world is in continuous flux as Buddhism often points out. This need for consistency supports the illusion of a solid self, unchanging and in control. But based on what we have learned so far, we might more accurately think of the self as a river whose form is in constant forward flow. Just so, our self is continuously changing by way of ideas, perceptions, and feelings.

In my class on consciousness, we do an exercise where we spend a whole day becoming aware of how many selves appear and disappear. You can do this too. On the surface, you might first notice a "work self" and then a "home self," but if you are attentive, even these will change moment to moment. At work, one self may come online with one coworker; then another self appears as a different coworker enters the room. If you shatter a glass in the break room, your irritation or embarrassment may bring another self forward, until you get an email that a meeting was suddenly canceled to the great relief of yet another self.

Sometimes I like to think of the singular "you" as a flip-book. If you take a stack of paper and draw a picture that slightly changes on each page and then flip through the pages, the still images will appear as a short animation. In reality, there are one hundred different pictures, but the mind weaves these together into one continuous story.

For this exploration, take a day and see if you can notice your shifting selves. Count the yous as they come and go.

Noting just how many "yous" appear in a day works to dismantle the illusion of a singular "you" behind it all. A sense of freedom can emerge from the realization that you are under no obligation to be consistent. You need not try to glue the continuous change in the world into one single thing. Anger may appear with one "you," but that is only one page of the flip-book, which will soon be replaced with another emotion, another perception, another thought. Like the sun rising and setting, these "yous" will come and go. There is no need to cling to some and avoid others. There need be no conflict between these selves—so you can abandon the wrestling match between "sinner you" and "saint you." This frees up an enormous amount of mental energy and fundamentally changes how we can experience the world.

Lastly, you can try to notice that in between the yous there are moments when you are so engaged in some activity that the self isn't even noticeably around. This points to a central question of this book: where is the self when no one is thinking about it?

FOUR

The Basics of Right-Brain Consciousness

Silence is the language of god,
all else is poor translation.

—Rumi

In December 1996, the history of neuroscience was forever changed when Dr. Jill Bolte Taylor suffered a stroke that took much of her left brain off-line.[1] In what must be a grand, cosmic coincidence, this event happened to a neuroanatomist. In other words, Taylor was someone who had spent her life before the stroke labeling and categorizing the brain, using the very part of her brain that would be, for the first time, turned off—opening up center stage for her right-brain consciousness.

Years later, after recovering from the injury, Taylor's left brain was able to tell the story. During the stroke, her constant inner voice was silent for the first time. As the inner language quieted, she reports, "I became detached from the memories of my life, [and] I was confronted by an expanding sense of grace." She could no longer perceive the boundaries of where she ended and everything else began. She felt her being as fluid rather than solid. She was totally in the present moment, embodied in tranquility. Categories such as good/bad and right/wrong were experienced as a continuum rather than disconnected opposites. Her left-brain ego, which viewed herself as separate, was no longer dominant in her consciousness. In her right brain (or perhaps her "right mind"?), she felt gratitude and a sense of contentment. The right brain was compassionate, nurturing, and eternally optimistic. In her words, "I think the Buddhists would say I entered the mode of existence they call nirvana."

It is important to point out that neuroscience is still trying to make sense of exactly what Taylor's experience means insofar as our understanding of the brain. However, one cannot help but wonder—as she did—whether her experience was similar to that of the Buddha, Lao-tzu, or the ancient Hindus that wrote the Vedas. In some ways, her experience is exactly what many people hope to attain when they meditate or practice mindfulness.

Of course, no one would sign up to experience a life-threatening stroke as a means to enlightenment. A more practical approach might be in this question: what would happen if we could "turn down" the left brain? Would this mean that the left brain could no longer inhibit the right brain? Perhaps this right-brain bliss is always on, and we are just not identifying with it? If you are familiar with Buddhism, you may have heard the expression that "you are already a buddha, you just don't know it." Based on what happened to Taylor, we might surmise that these right-brain processes are already being carried out to some degree; we just need to connect to or identify with them somehow, or perhaps we simply need to wake up to them. After all, *buddha* simply means "one that is awake."

It took years of rehabilitation to bring Taylor's left brain back to a functioning level, so even after this experience of bliss, she still worked very hard so that her left brain would function. She still needed it to move through the world and to continue her work. Perhaps the future of our happiness depends on finding a balance for the left-brain interpreter. In my view, the goal is not right-brain dominance and certainly not to shut down the left brain, but rather to achieve what the Buddha called a middle path.

Could Jill Bolte Taylor poststroke illustrate a living example of this balanced path? She talks about how she can now choose to enter right-brain bliss, a place she good-naturedly calls "la-la land," but she can also focus on left-brain processing to get things done, communicate with others, and solve the practical problems that come up in life.

A Closer Look at the Right Side of the Brain

After focusing on the left brain, it is now time to delve into the right side of the brain and see if what neuroscience has learned about this hemisphere also supports the idea that the self is a fiction.

Of course, this is also where we run into a dilemma. Since you are likely not a split-brain patient reading this book in a controlled experiment, both sides of your brain will be receiving the information presented next. Because of this, I encourage you to notice when the left brain—which wants to be the master of the conversation—dismisses any of the ideas presented next as "unimportant," "meaningless," or "silly" or otherwise looks for some way to reject them and maintain its dominance.

Remember that even though your right brain can't speak in the traditional sense, it does understand language on its own, as the case studies with the split-brain patients demonstrated. The extent that you understand the ideas presented here will of course rely on my ability to explain them, but could also be indicative of your ability to move beyond identification with the left-brain interpreter. So let's take a closer look at the speechless right brain, because as you will soon see, it is a fitting example of the age-old axiom that wisdom is often found in silence.

In many ways the right brain is the yin to the yang of the left brain.

For instance, in the same way that the left brain is categorical, the right brain takes a more global approach to what it perceives. Rather than dividing things into categories and making judgments that separate the world, the right brain gives attention to the whole scene and processes the world as a continuum. Whereas the attention of the left brain is focused and narrow, the right brain is broad, vigilant, and attends to the big picture. Whereas the left brain focuses on the local elements, the right brain processes the global form that the elements create.[2] The left brain is sequential, separating time into "before that" or "after this," while the right brain is focused on the immediacy of the present moment. The experience described by Taylor begins to make sense when we understand how the right brain processes information.

Another way to summarize the differences between the left and right brain is that the left brain is the language center and the right brain is the spatial center.

While admittedly this is reductive, it is a helpful way to summarize decades of research. Language is categorical; it looks at one word at a time with a narrow focus either as you read or as you speak. When we process the space around us, we deal with the whole at once, not individual parts but how the parts are all connected as they are in any picture.

To see the effects of this spatial processing, consider the next image.

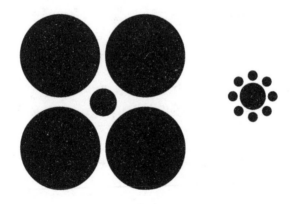

Which center circle looks larger? The vast majority of people who view this will say the center circle on the right looks larger. As you've probably guessed, this illusion works because the left brain is processing, categorizing, and comparing the data to make a guess. The interpreter is creating an abstraction based on categorical differences such as larger and smaller. In reality, both center circles are the same size, but the left looks smaller since it is compared to the categorically larger circles around it, while the center circle on the right looks larger compared to the categorically smaller circles that surround it.

On the other hand, in a clever study that demonstrates the accuracy of the right brain's spatial processing, researchers presented subjects with blocks of different sizes to replicate the above illusion.[3] Subjects were carefully videotaped as they were asked to reach out and grab the center block in each cluster, and the right brain performed perfectly. Even if the left brain "thought" the center blocks were different sizes, the right brain held the thumb and fingers the exact same distance apart. That is, the right brain wasn't fooled by the illusion like "you" are.

This experiment also leads us to another vital misunderstanding about the right brain. The subjects in this experiment didn't think about their fingers being the same distance apart as they reached for each circle, the choice was unconscious as far as the left brain was concerned. This label of "unconscious" is inherently negative in scientific usage and is a subtle way the left brain asserts its role as master. The effects of this label can be seen across multiple disciplines.

For instance, bodily and mental functions that don't require conscious thought or interpretation have largely been deemed of lesser importance by Western science and philosophy. But it's important to note that *philosophers and neuroscientists have labeled these things "unconscious" simply because they are outside of the language sphere*, even though they are still complex neurological behaviors. Think of your cardiovascular system or your digestive system as basic examples. They are doing very complex things all the time—things that could not be done without the brain—but because their actions are beyond the realm of the left brain thinking, they aren't paid much attention by the interpreter. But much like the functioning of these vital and necessary systems, the right brain's activities are just a form of consciousness that we've been taught to dismiss and devalue—not surprisingly, by the left brain.

You can experience this for yourself right now. Take a moment and raise your arm above your head. How did you do that? Can you explain it? Do you have to think about *how* to move your arm or do you just move it? To say that the very act of movement is somehow unconscious is to make thinking the master, yet thinking is not necessary for movement. Sure, you can think to yourself, "I would like to move my arm now," but the act itself needs no mental support.

Next I'd like you to reach out for any object near you and grab hold of it. This demonstrates your ability to accurately determine the distance between things in space—their spatial reality. Did you grab something without any problem? Or did your hand reach out and miss the item altogether? Most likely it was the former. Now, how much did you think about this as far as traditional interpretive consciousness is concerned? Can you explain to me *how* you grabbed it? Here again, thinking wasn't required; you just did it. Because there is no story necessary for reaching out and grabbing something, it seems as if you were not conscious of how this is done due to our bias of identifying with a language-based interpretive consciousness. However it's important to notice that these examples—either moving your arm above your head or grabbing an object in front of you—are both highly complex and conscious activities even though they are outside the language sphere. They are simply given very little importance, because the left brain enjoys playing the master.

Because we don't have words to even describe how we do movement, many will consider it meaningless to ask if it is conscious. The most common answer from my students to the question "how did you do that?" is a blank look and the response, "I don't know, I just did it." Dismissing this action as unconscious is a result of our overdependence on the language-based interpretative consciousness our interpretive pattern perceiver cannot imagine a world without.

Experiencing Right-Brain Consciousness

So how can one become more conscious of the right-brain system? Well, in one sense you already are quite conscious of it, but the bias of seeing the world mostly through the lens of the interpreter only makes it *seem* like you're not. Of course, when I say "you," I don't mean your ego, because the ego genuinely cannot experience the right-brain consciousness even if it wants to, as it is a left-brain construct only. Although there are many ways to access consciousness of right-brain activity, due to the lack of labels and words it can be difficult to express this form of consciousness. Still, let's look at a few of them quickly.

The practice of yoga, which has been around for thousands of years and is mentioned in the oldest religious texts of India, brings you into right-brain consciousness. You are doing movements, you typically feel good when you do them, you are aware of what you are doing, but there is very little to "think" about. In fact the whole practice is best done by "being in the moment" or not getting lost in the machinations of the interpreter while you are doing it. I can't think of a single practitioner of yoga who would ever believe that one is unconscious during this practice. I also find it interesting that the word *yoga* means "union," the union of your true self and the rest of the universe.

The practice of meditation in its various forms also brings you into right-brain consciousness. Zazen, or the seated meditation practiced in most Zen schools, often instructs beginners to become conscious of their breath, which brings their attention into the present moment. Another thing to note here is that for most people, breathing happens, but we aren't "conscious" of it in that we pay no attention to it. There's nothing to "think" about when we breathe, and that's another reason why so many meditation practices may accentuate it. Also consider the moving forms of meditation: tai chi and qigong. These ancient Eastern practices are done to increase chi, or internal energy. While each can take a lifetime to master, the basics are pretty simple, and they both involve movement shifts from the left to the right and back again with movements coordinated to breathing. When done well, one is conscious of movement within space without verbal labels.

No one would say that any of these practices are unconscious; rather many describe them as a very alert form of consciousness that is difficult to put into words. However, just because something cannot be put into words does not make it unconscious. This echoes the wisdom of the ancient Eastern philosophers, who said that the real world couldn't be put into words and anything put into words was not the real world.

It may be that right-brain consciousness is also what happens when one is "in the zone." Basketball player Michael Jordan popularized this phrase because it is how he described making basket after basket without thinking about it. Others may find this state naturally while engaged in certain activities that don't rely on conscious thought, such as playing a musical instrument, engaging in physical activity, being creative in some form, praying or meditating, or even fixing a motorcycle—as in the classic novel *Zen and the Art of Motorcycle Maintenance* by Robert M. Pirsig.

Being in the zone is very similar to what psychologist Mihaly Csikszentmihalyi has called *flow*, using this term to describe the experience that someone has while being totally absorbed in the doing of something. He defines flow as: "Being completely involved in an activity for its own sake. The ego falls away. Time flies. Every action, movement, and thought follows inevitably from the previous one, like playing jazz. Your whole being is involved, and you're using your skills to the utmost."[4] On a side note, it is funny that he picked jazz as an example because as the great musician Louis Armstrong put it, "If you have to ask what jazz is, you'll never know."

After being in the zone or flow, interpretive consciousness will sometimes look back and either take credit for these experiences ("I" did great) or dismiss them as unimportant, both of which are subtle ways it maintains its superiority as master. You likely experience right-brain consciousness all the time, but because the "master" has control over language and language can be a very convincing tool, the "master" takes credit for these experiences or pays no attention to them. Imagine the right brain on the stand in court being questioned by a left-brain lawyer. How does the right brain convince the jury that it is conscious when all the rules of the game have been constructed by the linguistic left brain?

Finally, another well-known way to experience right-brain consciousness is the practice of mindfulness, something that is most often associated with Buddhism and other Eastern traditions. Mindfulness in this context is defined as being fully in the present moment, observing what is happening in the world around you along with the world inside you—your thoughts, feelings, sensations. Practitioners are often taught to watch the machinations of the mind without attaching too much importance to them in the form of a judgment—which, if you remember, is one strength of the left brain. Mindfulness teachers explain that when a thought arises, one can notice it rather than attaching to it, bringing one's attention back to the present moment rather than following that thought chain into a story about reality. The practice of mindfulness is about being in and observing reality rather than thinking about reality—like being a watcher of events in the present, both inside and outside. This begs the question, who is doing the watching? Could it be the right-brain consciousness? We will return to this question, but in the meantime we can see that practicing mindfulness is a way of being in the world that lessens your identification with the left-brain interpreter. Because our interpreter is so constant, we have to *practice* being mindful.

All of these examples of right-brain consciousness are focused on experiences in the present moment and in doing and being in a way that is beyond thinking and language. The right brain acts in a way that agrees with the Nike slogan "Just Do It," and I'm convinced it would yell this out if it could. You don't learn how to play an instrument by reading about what the instrument is; you have to practice. You don't make a basket in basketball by thinking about it; you have to do it. And you can only do it in the present moment.

One could say that the essence of the right-brain consciousness is this: it does things without thinking about them, by which I mean without language or thought. This makes it difficult to write about—and even think about!

I will sometimes ask students, "What percentage of your existence is spent doing versus thinking?" I give them a moment to consider, and then I tell them that it's a bit of a trick question, since your thinking mind is doing the evaluating. This question reminds me of the old saying "You can't get there from here." That is absolutely true when it comes to peering into the right-brain system from the left-brain system. Even if the left brain wants to go beyond itself, it can only go deeper into itself.

I experienced this myself in my first martial arts sparring match. I scored a quick point because I wasn't thinking . . . I was just doing. Then, when I started thinking how cool it would be to win, my performance quickly diminished. It wasn't *what* I was thinking that negatively impacted my performance; it was the fact that I was thinking at all.

Perhaps this is why the ancient Eastern philosophers valued nonlinguistic consciousness to a degree that is difficult for modern Westerners to appreciate. Again, neuropsychology is catching up to this, but it hasn't exactly gotten there yet. Consider the following quote from the Advaita Vedanta master Nisargadatta Maharaj: "In your world, the unspoken has no existence. In mine the words and their contents have no being. . . . My world is real, while yours is made of dreams." To live in a world of abstractions—based on language, concepts, beliefs, patterns, labels—is to live in a dream world rather than reality.

One of the primary teachings of Zen Buddhism is to bring your consciousness back to reality, saving it from being lost in the world of the abstract. When my class gets too lost in one abstraction after another, I will clap my hands together making a noise loud enough to startle students sleeping in the back. I remind them that at that point, for the moment they were startled by the clap, they were awake without thought: that is Zen.

At my son's soccer match, I found myself in a conversation with another soccer dad about how stressful work was at the time. I tried to explain that most stress is the result of taking fictitious stories too seriously, but he was having a hard time separating the story (left-brain interpreting) from the reality (right-brain witnessing). So, I pointed to the soccer field and reminded him that there was no soccer championship going on "out there," there were no teams "out there," no points were being scored outside of the collective fiction in our heads. The only thing "out there" was a bunch of little boys running around kicking a ball, and everything else made up our story about it. In the reality of the right brain, there are no winners or losers, no teams or champion-ships, there is just being and doing. After I explained all of that, he stared at me with a blank expression and quickly changed the subject.

Think of this soccer tournament. Beyond the being and doing of boys kicking a ball on a field, it is all a story. Winners, losers, championships—these are all based on categories, labels, patterns. Language and thought provide the tools to generate these stories. Our whole lives, even our very sense of self, might be thought of in the same way as this soccer game. The abstract sto-ries themselves aren't the problem, but becoming lost in them *creates* the problem. Our suffering comes from getting swept up in these stories and forgetting that they are not themselves reality.

In this way, the story is always an illusion; it only exists in the mind—and only when we are in the process of telling it in words or thoughts. Perhaps you can see that this is true not only of the story but also of the story-teller, the self, which is another very convincing illusion and exists only when someone is thinking about it.

We have barely scratched the surface of the right brain's amazing abilities. And remember: reading about the functions of the right brain isn't the same as experienc-ing them. Practices such as meditation, yoga, tai chi, and mindfulness are great places to start. Later we will aim to find a balanced approach that allows us to keep the benefits of the interpreter without getting lost in the story itself. Until then, we will keep exploring the right brain, unearthing some ways in which it could be considered smarter than the left brain. Read on carefully— or should I say mindfully—since your interpreter may not like this one bit . . .

Explorations
Just Doing It!

The right brain is the "doing it" center of the brain. One way to get more in touch with the right brain is to cut the left brain out of activities by doing them for no reason—not for money, not to improve oneself, but simply for the sake of doing them. The left-brain ego thinks in terms of cause and effect, and in order for an action to be worth taking, it must have a positive outcome, but this can complicate the actual doing of the tasks. Doing for its own purpose seems to almost always be connected with right-brain activities from poetry to art to music.

Once a day, do something for no reason at all. As one cannot plan to be spontaneous no matter what your left brain tells you, allow for moments of opportunity to arise. If at some point you feel like getting up and taking a walk, do so—not because you want the fresh air or because work is boring but because you had the inclination and now are acting upon it "for no reason."

Conscious Breathing

Close your eyes and become conscious of just one breath. With your attention focused on your body, draw air in slowly through your nose. Feel it filling your lungs, the sensation of your belly and chest expanding as you bring in fresh oxygen. Hold the breath for a single second. Be conscious of the tightness in your chest as you hold the breath, of the stillness around and inside of you. Release the breath slowly and in a controlled manner through your mouth. You may wish to make a sound such as "ahh" or "om" as you release the breath. In this way, by focusing on your body and the act of breathing, you wrest control away from the chattering left brain and allow yourself to explore a function that is normally delegated to the "unconscious" right brain. With even a single breath, you can turn this around and become the one that breathes.

This has become one of my favorite practices, because no matter how busy the left brain believes it is, there is always time for one conscious breath. Never underestimate the power of a single conscious breath to bring you out of a left-brain fantasy and back into the real world. And don't be surprised if one breath turns into two or three—just do it!

The BS Detector

Have you ever had an aha moment in which you got a lightning bolt of clarity about reality seemingly out of the blue?

The work of neuroscientist V. S. Ramachandran suggests that the right brain acts like a counterbalance or regulator to the constant storytelling of the left-brain interpreter and it "steps in" anytime the stories become too outlandish.[5]

People often report a shock that enables them to make a big change—whether it's breaking free from an abusive relationship or seeing the need for a career change. The story that made sense until that moment gets a big jolt. Ramachandran's work suggests that in this moment of realization, your right brain has let your left brain know, "Hey, your story is now too far away from reality." In this way, the right brain isn't "thinking" in the same way we equate this function with the left brain, but rather it is observing the evidence and signaling to the left brain it's time to wake up.

Interestingly, just like with the split-brain patients we looked at earlier in the book, the left brain may take credit for these instances and say things like, "I had a realization today," or "I experienced a moment of clarity." Of course the "I" in this sentence is the left-brain interpreter, and it was the cause of the problem rather than the solution. Meanwhile the right brain, devoid of ego and the need for credit, doesn't care—just as long as the change is made. When have you made similar realizations in your own life? Where do you think, or rather feel, that they came from in light of this research?

FIVE

Meaning and Understanding

To understand everything, is to forgive everything.
—Buddha

Meaning and understanding are two of the vital processes that take place in the right brain. This often surprises my students to hear, since the left brain seems to be the one doing all the thinking, but as you will see in this chapter, while the left brain focuses on the parts, the right brain looks at the whole where meaning and understanding reside. A good way to see this is through example, so let's do a quick exercise. Read the following paragraph from *Context and Memory* by M. Klein very carefully:

A newspaper is better than a magazine. A sea-shore is a better place than the street. At first it is better to run than to walk. You may have to try several times. It takes some skill but it is easy to learn. Even young children can enjoy it. Once successful, complications are minimal. Birds seldom get too close. Rain, however, soaks in very fast. Too many people doing the same thing can also cause problems. One needs lots of room. If there are no complications it can be very peaceful. A rock will serve as an anchor. If things break loose from it, however, you will not get a second chance.[1]

How does it feel? It doesn't feel quite right, does it? Maybe a bit random, or meaningless? Most likely, your interpretive consciousness took in each specific word, understanding individual definitions and yet not grasping any meaning that would glue it all together. Now, go back and read it again, this time with the understanding that the passage is about flying a kite. Now it all makes sense, doesn't it? The right side of the brain makes this possible.

Almost every cognitive task depends on meaning. Meaning allows us to hold information in short-term or long-term memory and thus is the foundation of cognition. For instance, imagine that you need to memorize one of the two sentences below. Which do you choose and why?

A. Martin Luther King Jr., winner of the Nobel Peace Prize, gave a speech about civil rights at the Lincoln Memorial.

B. Apple purple bench, seven whales in Texas flew south, oven rust runs faster when it slides on twenty-seven roads.

Each of the above has the same number of words, but most everyone would agree that *A* is much easier to hold in memory than *B*. That is because we can process it in meaningful chunks such that "Martin Luther King Jr." becomes one meaningful piece of information rather than many.[2] Because of meaning, *A* is easier to hold in memory.

When I see students in the hallways with cards trying to memorize facts for an exam, it takes everything I have not to burst into a lecture on the importance of meaning for both short-term and long-term memory. In the 1970s, psychology introduced a theory called "levels of processing," but it could very well be called "levels of meaning."[3] The theory was very simple: if you process the meaning, you will remember it, but if you process only the surface features by just reading it to yourself or looking at the words, it will be forgotten.

This happens all the time. The next time you have a book and actually want to remember what you've read,

read two or three paragraphs, close the book, and then ask yourself, "What did I just read?" You can do it right now. Close this book and say out loud what this chapter has covered so far. You may be surprised to find you are met with a blank nothingness because you were just processing the surface features. However, if you practice and ask yourself this question regularly as you read, you will get better at retaining meaning and creating long-term memories of what you read.

Finding meaning isn't just about improving your memorization skills, of course. Finding meaning may be the purpose of life itself. In one of the most powerful books showing the importance of meaning in the human condition, *Man's Search for Meaning*, psychiatrist Viktor Frankl describes his experiences in the Nazi death camps during WWII.[4] He begins with a quote from Friedrich Nietzsche, "He who has a why to live for can bear almost any how." Frankl contended that an inmate's sense of meaning and purpose was a factor in his or her ability to survive in the camps. Frankl concluded that meaning is more important than happiness and called his form of therapy *logotherapy* because *logos* translates as "meaning."

Frankl believed that it is "the very pursuit of happiness that thwarts happiness." Meanwhile, psychology—and much of culture—has been on a pursuit of happiness crusade for at least the last thirty years. However, the current research is backing up Frankl's insights. In one study, subjects listened to music while half of them tried as hard as they could to be happy.[5] The half that tried to be happy were *less happy* than the group that just listened. Another study found that those who put a high value on happiness had more negative emotions.[6] Of course, long ago the Buddha explained how desire leads to suffering; this seems to also hold even for the desire to be happy.

Any new parent can tell you that meaning is different than happiness. In fact, becoming a new parent is one of the clearest ways to trade ego happiness for meaning and never look back. In my own case, because I am no good for breastfeeding, my job as a new parent was changing diapers. I have changed thousands of diapers, and I vividly recall the array of fluids and solids that came my way during those first few years. My sleep was reduced to far less than half of what it had previously been. My moment-to-moment existence was outwardly miserable in many ways. Yet I wouldn't trade being a parent for anything in the world, then or now. Only meaning could ever make such a deal worth being grateful for.

Or to put it another way, if you have a why, you can deal with any how.

Understanding

Many of us are told that to think about something is to understand it, so at first glance understanding is often equated with the left brain. This is what I call "interpretive understanding," as it focuses on how separate things cause each other to happen. There is another kind of understanding that is related to our discussion on meaning, and it depends on a broader view of a whole system of happenings. Let's look at both types of understanding to see how they differ.

The writings of Isaac Newton, whose work forms the foundation of modern science, follows a pattern of interpretive understanding. For instance, many Westerners still view the universe as a vast machine, similar to a clock. A simple mechanical clock has a few gears, a power supply, and a winding system, which all work together to make some hands move around on a dial. Imagine you understood the details about each piece of a clock and how they work together. You could put together and take apart gears and dials, but might never know what a watch is or does. It is the same with the universe—the narrow window of interpretive consciousness is only aware of one thing at a time and totally in the dark about the glue that binds it all together. Seeking a true understanding of a clock—or of the universe—is like reading the previous passage on flying a kite: it requires something more than the individual parts.

A classic example given by Newton is one billiard ball hitting another. We can *see* one ball hitting the next, and it has a nice one-thing-at-a-time quality. *A* hits *B* and then *B* moves. Every part of the transaction can be described with words, and anything that cannot be described with words is off limits. When we describe Newton's version of the universe as one ball causing another to move, the left brain might say, "I understand." Why does my car make a strange noise? The muffler went bad and needs to be replaced. Why do I have a pain in my stomach? There is too much acid, and I need to take medicine to fix it. In fact, this one thing causing something else is at the core of science and a reflection of how the interpretive mind works to break the world into parts, categories, and differences. The left brain does this, all the while never grasping that none of it would be possible without the powers of the right brain to guide and make sense of the whole enterprise.

This is not to say that the simple left-brain form of understanding isn't ever in agreement with reality. Sometimes, if I replace the muffler in my car, the sound does go away. If I take an antacid, my stomach does feel better. This form of understanding has been instrumental in those breakthroughs that gave us flight, took us to the moon, and now has us moving about in cars that drive themselves.

While seeing one thing at a time is a necessary and useful process, it is fundamentally dependent on the larger vision taking place in the right brain. This is ironic when you consider how the left brain masquerades as the master. We need the right brain to understand the purpose of a car or our digestive system, and only then can we focus on the specific parts that construct these larger processes.

Metaphor

Let's try and put this together in a model that the left brain can understand better—because your right brain already gets it. A good way to do that is through metaphor and simile (the latter being a form of metaphor). In order for metaphor to mean anything at all, one must be able to make connections that are not apparent while focusing on the linear parts only.

For instance, in trying to first describe what love is, one might say, "Love is like a rose: beautiful but with thorns that can hurt sometimes." At work we can "get ahead," "fall behind," or "make it to the top." In these metaphors we are mapping an abstraction onto a perception. While metaphors call on both the left and right brain, here again it is the left that relies on the right.

Metaphors make connections that are beyond literal meaning—even if the left brain sometimes takes them to be literal. Imagine if someone offered you an idea that was "food for thought" but you refused, explaining that you just ate.

Similarly, thinking that the universe is a clocklike machine might be a useful metaphor. Given free rein with this metaphor, however, the left brain might lead us straight down a literal path to a tragic conclusion: what if we are also only a machine within an ever larger, lifeless machine? This line of thinking will most certainly lead to suffering.

Equating perception with understanding is the essence of metaphor; we take something abstract and connect it to a right-brain experience, hoping that the left brain will get it. There is a large body of research showing the right brain is critical in metaphor and that individuals with damage to the right brain will take poems, metaphors, and sarcasm literally.[7] To take a metaphor literally is to miss the connection.

There is a long tradition in both philosophy and religion of using metaphors in the quest for understanding, especially in the East. The Pali Canon is the collection of writings typically considered the best record of the Buddha's teachings. This text includes over a thousand metaphors.[8] In Buddhism, the mind is like a pool because its water clears when left alone, and the "middle path" conveys moderation. Even the phrase "the Buddha" is grounded in metaphor, because the original Pali term simply means "one who is awake." If taken literally, this would mean that anyone who isn't sleeping is a buddha, though of course being *awake* in this context means being conscious of reality rather than hypnotized by our dreamlike stories about reality.

With metaphor, the brain is making a connection between a pattern of neural activity and the real, genuine world. Metaphor is also the very heart of poetry. As Emily Dickinson writes, "Hope is the thing with feathers." There is no hope in taking this literally, but the right brain sees the unusual way in which hope and feathers are connected. In this sense, perception itself is like poetry and our most basic conscious experiences are like writing a poem.

Perhaps the reason Buddhism and other spiritual traditions use metaphors so frequently is because they sidestep the gatekeeping functions of the interpretive mind. On the surface, most metaphors seem simple and innocent, so the interpreter doesn't engage any of its defenses. By the time the right brain is active, experience has already transcended the left brain to some degree.

Unlike the verbal silence that is going on in the right brain, the vast majority of happenings in the left side are ideas about other ideas, or ideas about ideas about ideas, in a sort of self-generated bureaucratic machine. Of course, these stories and interpretations are all abstractions, so one could say that what is going on in the left brain is countless images reflected in water with no substance. Or, as a Zen Buddhist might say, "the mind is like water."

Spatial Processing

As mentioned in the last chapter, the right brain is key in spatial processing. Rather than focusing on one thing at a time, the right brain senses the whole picture— both the things themselves and the spaces in between. One could say that the right brain understands that a figure is determined by its background; something the left brain tends to overlook.

The truth is that no figure could exist without the background and the shape of the background is dependent upon the figure. This is so simple that you might miss the fundamental importance of it, especially if you are overidentifying with the left brain. For instance, let's go back to kindergarten for a moment and think of something as simple as the difference between the idea of one and two. What is this difference? It isn't a thing that turns one into two but rather the space between. A space between one creates two.

I I

And what is the difference between two and three?

I I I

Again, just more space. And what is four, but adding more space? Things are intrinsically linked to space. Space connects. Space creates all things. Yet if you remember the quick exercise we did in chapter 1, the left-brain interpreter only focused on the objects in a room and you likely did not even consider the empty space when listing what you saw.

The yin-yang symbol of Taoism expresses this truth perfectly. The white is necessary to see the black and the black is necessary to see the white. There is an understanding here that can't be grasped by the left brain, a message these ancient masters conveyed to us with an image.

Just as the background defines the figure, space defines all the things in the world, because space is the ultimate background. Without space, or emptiness, no separate things could exist. This suggests why Buddhism, particularly Zen Buddhism, has such a romance with emptiness and space, because these things make everything else possible. Consider this section from the Heart Sutra of Mahayana Buddhism:

Form is emptiness, emptiness is form
Emptiness is not separate from form
Form is not separate from emptiness
Whatever is form is emptiness
Whatever is emptiness is form

Often said to be "Buddhism in a nutshell," this excerpt is used to meditate around the interconnected ideas of emptiness and form in a way that brings the two together, rather than creating categorical separations.

Consider the act of reading: The words on this page are so interdependent on their surroundings that we cannot separate the word and its background. The words only stand out because they are different from the background. The space between the lines and curves that make up the letters are equally as important as the letters themselves. In a way, it is almost as if the space is *more* important, since it is the space between the parts that creates the difference between one word and everything else.

If reality were an ocean, the left brain could only take in one wave at a time. The right brain sees the vastness of the sea all at once. Both of these are a kind of image of reality rather than reality itself. No matter how the ocean is taken in, the ocean does not change its nature; only its appearance changes. But because the right brain is sensing the entire picture including the empty space, rather than just the objects in space one at a time as the left brain does, reality is more closely represented in the right brain. The right brain senses the world in parallel (all at once), while the left brain senses the world in series (one thing at a time).

It is standard in psychology to refer to parallel forms of processing as unconscious, in exactly the same way it treats digestive and respiratory systems as unconscious. Again, the left brain is considered the "master" of reality, and the right brain is portrayed as unconscious. I hope that you are now starting to realize that this is simply not the case. Rather, the right brain is a form of consciousness that does not rely on words. According to Eastern philosophical schools, not relying on words is a wonderful way to be—and might well decrease the suffering of humankind.

Explorations
Space Exercise for Consciousness
Moving from Earth into outer space can have the effect of directing consciousness out of the interpretive mind, as astronaut and moonwalker Edgar Mitchell noted. "What I experienced during that three-day trip home was nothing short of an overwhelming sense of universal connectedness. I actually felt what has been described

as an ecstasy of unity. . . . I perceived the universe as in some way conscious. The thought was so large it seemed inexpressible, and to a large degree it still is."[9]

It's a little ironic that we need to go into outer space to appreciate the power of the space that we have not only failed to notice, but also failed to notice that we have failed to notice. There seems to be agreement among scientists that only 5 percent of our universe is made up of what we might consider typical matter. So perhaps in outer space, it just becomes more obvious that space is more prevalent than matter. Stuck on the familiar perspective of Earth's landscape, the left brain can more easily tell the story that matter is more important.

For this exercise, I invite you to redirect awareness to the space between your hands, the space between you and the next person you see, the space between any objects in front of you now. There is so much space that there are infinite variations of this practice, and you don't have to leave Earth to experience it. One practice is to look outward into the night sky and focus on the space between things. There is something about space that slows the mind, since the mind has no way to understand it because it has no content and no container. Therefore, when we shift our awareness to it, the interpretive mind slows down.

The Silence In Between

Without space no thing is possible, and without silence no sound is possible. Noticing how the sounds of many things depend on the silence in the background can be very helpful in exploring the concepts we've been covering. When you listen to someone speak, or when you speak yourself, bring some attention to the silent space between the sounds. Can you sense in the same way a figure is dependent on the background that sound is dependent on silence? Without silence, sound would have no meaning.

Consider how these two explorations relate to the Buddhist mantra form is void, void is form.

SIX

Right-Brain Intelligence— Intuition, Emotions, and Creativity

The intuitive mind is a sacred gift and the rational mind is a faithful servant. We have created a society that honors the servant and has forgotten the gift.
—Albert Einstein

Zen Buddhism has a teaching called *prajnaparamita*, which is typically translated as "the perfection of wisdom." It's important to point out that the wisdom referred to here is not the same as intellectual knowledge, but a type of insight into the nature of reality that is beyond language and reasoning. *Prajna* is also referred to in Zen writings as "wisdom beyond wisdom." This kind of wisdom is very much connected to the teaching on emptiness we reviewed at the end of the last chapter, since this type of wisdom allows you to make the connection between empty space and matter.

Given the emphasis on nonverbal knowing, I can't help but wonder if the wisdom referred to in *prajna-paramita* can only be understood by the right brain. While we may never have a definitive answer to this question, one thing is certain: there is a source of intelligence in the right brain that is beyond the capacity of the left-brain interpreter to understand, and modern neuroscience is not the first to notice this.

Over one hundred years ago, the famous American psychologist William James wrote about a nonsensory type of intelligence he called "fringe consciousness," which according to James describes a vague "feeling of knowing" that doesn't seem to have a direct sensory or perceptual content to it.[1] For instance, if you've ever walked into a particular room for the first time and just felt it to be a great place to hang out; this experience is fringe consciousness. The idea is that you are simultaneously processing the whole room at once—the music, the art on the walls, the furniture, and the relations between the parts—into one vague feeling that you like it. One possible way to explain this experience is to say that because interpretive consciousness is so limited, the fringe works by processing the whole context and then produces a general feeling of rightness or wrongness, sort of a summary statement about the big picture or all things collectively.[2]

Some of my favorite examples of fringe consciousness experiences from my own life have happened when I have left the house and remembered that I've forgotten something but can't think of what it is or when I have spotted someone I had met previously and just couldn't remember their name, despite being sure I knew it. James called these types of experiences tip-of-the-tongue events, since it is as if the content were right there but, because I can't say it, I can't quite produce that content. Students will often say that they know the answer on a test but simply *can't prove it right now*.

Brain-imaging research has shown that during the tip-of-the-tongue moment, it is the right brain that "lights up."[3] And as you will see in this chapter, the right brain carries most of the weight for these nonverbal types of knowing, and one of the most interesting examples of this—and the most unexplained by Western science—is what we commonly refer to as *intuition*.

Intuition

Merriam-Webster's Dictionary defines *intuition* as "immediate apprehension or cognition without reasoning," and "gaining direct knowledge or cognition without evident rational thought and inference." Based on this definition, you can see that intuition presents quite a quandary for the left-brain interpreter.

With intuition, knowing happens without explicitly being able to put into words how you know or from where this knowing comes. You have likely experienced this in your own life in big and little ways. For instance, the forecast may be for sun all day, but something tells you that you'd better bring an umbrella. Then when a "freak" thunderstorm rolls in in the afternoon, you say, "I knew it!" Intuition might lead a close friend or relative to know someone they care about is hurt or in trouble without ever receiving a phone call or text to that effect. There are several reported examples of people making lifesaving decisions because they followed their intuition, and science and psychology are unable to explain how this works—which only means that they can't explain it via the left-brain interpreter.

Often, intuition is dismissed as being "just a coincidence," but James saw that these experiences were too common to be explained as pure chance, but rather pointed to something that was occurring within us that the conscious mind wasn't fully aware of—hence, the name of fringe. Not surprisingly, those who highly identify with the left-brain interpreter will typically conclude that intuition is either silly or superstitious. While the interpretive mind doesn't trust intuition, I think intuition is another valid form of consciousness that the "master" has devalued, and as a result many people have either lost touch with or don't trust this aspect of our consciousness.

There have been some recent scientific studies regarding intuition that have measured this "nonconscious" (i.e., not available to the left brain's language sphere) decision-making and support the idea that intuition is a form of intelligence that in some ways is superior to left-brain knowledge.

In one study, participants were presented with two stacks of cards, two thousand dollars, and a game in which the object was to win as much money as possible.[4] They could choose a card from either stack and receive an immediate financial win or loss. The first stack had big wins but also big losses, and the second stack had small wins but almost no losses. Overall, playing from the second deck was the most advantageous. Here's the interesting part: It took fifty to eighty draws of cards before most subjects became "conscious" (meaning they noticed it with their left brain) of the how the decks were rigged. However, researchers were also measuring the participants' sweat glands, and they recorded that their palms produced sweat, a sign of nervousness, every time they reached for the first deck after only ten cards. This meant that an unconscious intelligence arrived at the correct conclusion much earlier than the left-brain interpreter.

Even more interestingly, a handful of participants never consciously figured out that deck two was the best way to win, but even these participants experienced sweaty palms when reaching for the riskier deck. So for these participants, the right brain was aware of the correct choices and the left brain never caught up.[5]

In another study designed to measure intuition's effect on decision-making, participants were presented with a video monitor that at first displayed only random dots similar to what would be described as snow on an old TV.[6] Unbeknownst to the participants' conscious minds, the researchers flashed emotion-provoking images, such as cute puppies (positive) or scary snakes (negative), and then asked participants to indicate if the dots were moving left or right on the screen—not an easy task, given the subtleties of the movement. The type of image shown also correlated to the direction of the dots, so that positive images meant the dots moved one way and negative images meant the dots moved another. The results were striking.[7] Participants made much faster and more accurate decisions about the direction of the dots when the emotional images were appearing in the background. Remember these images were unavailable to the interpreter, which never realized they were there.

This study makes sense in the context of the right brain seeing the whole picture rather than just the parts and being aware of things that aren't apparent to the left-brain interpreter.[8] It then influences the choices of the left brain, even without the left brain being aware of why it's making these choices. Perhaps this is intuition in a nutshell: the right brain senses information that isn't available to the left-brain interpreter and sends it over in the form of what is described as an inspiration or gut feeling that the left brain can't quite put into words and so it has reached the end of its ability to understand how it knows what it knows.

Emotions

The right side of the brain is also the region primarily responsible for emotions—from joy to grief, happiness to sadness, and everything in between. This connection between intuition, emotion, and our physical bodies is apparent in the metaphor that describes intuitive nudges as "gut feelings." In Western society, we are often told to choose "logic over emotion," which is another way the left-brain interpreter demands to play master.

Most intelligence tests measure verbal ability and reasoning, so if your vocabulary is extensive, you will be at the top of the traditional IQ food chain. Of course, you could lack social intelligence, empathy, and even self-awareness, but these are largely unmeasured on such tests in a left-brain-dominated culture. You may even know someone who seems "so smart you can't have a normal conversation with them," which speaks to the way we currently measure intelligence.

Fortunately, this all began to change in the mid-1990s when Daniel Goleman popularized the idea of emotional intelligence or EQ (emotional quotient) in his book of the same name.[9] EQ is defined as one's ability to recognize, understand, and manage their own emotions, as well as recognizing and understanding the emotions of others. In Goleman's more recent book, he looked at EQ and the brain and views EQ as consisting of four parts or elements: self-awareness, self-management, social awareness, and relationship management.[10] He also references four areas of the brain deeply involved in EQ—mostly on the right side. While it may be more obvious that we "feel" our way around in the last two parts of EQ, it might be more unusual to think about how self-awareness and self-management fit into this, so let me explain.

A little after *Emotional Intelligence* came out, I published a research article on how individuals with greater influence from the right side of the brain are more self-reflective.[11] The idea is pretty simple. If the left side of the brain creates an image of who we think we are (our egos), then the only way to reflect on this idea is from outside the system, which is the right brain. However, the right brain "speaks" only in emotions, so with self-reflection, we feel our way around thinking to find out what is true for us in a particular situation.

One could argue that Zen Buddhists were some of the first to work at increasing EQ. While some may think that a Zen master is devoid of emotion, this is not true. It's not about lacking emotion; rather, one could say that they have mastered their emotions because they do not fight them and in this way they are free from them. There is an old Zen story about a student with an anger problem that illustrates this perfectly. The story goes that when the student expressed concern about his own bad temper to his master, the master said, "Show it to me." Of course, the student couldn't and explained that it wasn't within his control to produce it at will, but rather it just happened. The master replied that if it wasn't within his control, then it was not part of his true nature. From that point on, whenever the student felt anger welling up inside of him, he recalled the master's words and his anger began to subside.

The advice to watch your emotions as they happen can increase your EQ because it puts space between the interpretive reaction and the emotion. It also teaches us not to fight or try and suppress our emotions, which is always a losing battle. Zen meditation instructs that when a distracting thought or emotion arises while meditating, one notices it and returns to the present moment.

Consider the natural flow of emotions in an infant—nothing is forced, and there are no "good" or "bad" emotions because there are no learned categories and no language. Years later, we judge that some emotions are good and should be sought out, while others are bad and should be avoided. In psychology, this eventually turned into the happiness movement, where people were desperately trying to find happiness by avoiding any and all negative emotions. Of course nothing could be further from the practice of Zen. In Zen, there is no such thing as a wrong emotion, and therefore nothing to strive for or fight against. My students know very well not to tell me to "have a nice day" because there is nothing wrong with a bad day or a bad mood.

During a now famous lecture, the Eastern philosopher and spiritual teacher J. Krishnamurti asked the audience "Do you want to know what my secret is?" According to several accounts of this story, in a soft voice, he said, "I don't mind what happens."

In the absolute acceptance of all emotions, they no longer have control over you because you have given up trying to control them. Perhaps a more accurate way to say this is that the interpretive mind has given up trying to control emotions, and in this way it is no longer attempting to be master.

Gratitude and Compassion

Two emotions that can give us a special window into the right brain are gratitude and compassion. Most people agree these are virtuous traits that can help us live a more fulfilling life, and so we have come to understand them as ideals to strive for or attributes that one must "achieve." However, gratitude and compassion are innate in our being, as the experience of Dr. Jill Bolte Taylor, whom we met in a previous chapter, suggests.

Taylor reported that during her stroke ordeal she felt extremely compassionate and eternally optimistic. Because her stroke took her left brain off-line, these feelings could only have come from her right brain, and this suggests that gratitude and compassion are already programmed into us. Perhaps we find them difficult to access amid the chatter of the left-brain interpreter. While some accuse optimists of "living in a fantasy world," being grateful is actually a deep appreciation for reality. Some studies have shown that feelings of gratitude activate the right side of the brain. But before we look at those, let's examine the opposite of gratitude, complaining, and where this may occur in the brain.

Complaining is a popular and well-accepted form of social interaction. I don't mean being skeptical or offering constructive criticism—those can be very helpful. By complaining, I mean *objecting to things as they are* in a way that isn't helpful, such as, "this cloudy weather is terrible!"

For our purposes, let's define complaints as statements that advocate the idea that things "shouldn't be the way they are" or that "this shouldn't have happened." As you can probably guess, whether said out loud or just in your head, complaints always stem from the interpretive mind. A complaint is strictly an interpretation of events, a story, and a negative judgment.

For instance, statements such as "This rain is ruining my day," or "I can't believe I got a flat tire," or "Traffic is horrible," are all examples reflecting a negative mind-set rather than helpful criticism. We even have a popular conversational game in our culture—the "worst day" competition, in which people argue about who had the worst day and in some strange way the winner is the real loser.

As you can imagine—and numerous studies have confirmed this—complaining leads to increased levels of anxiety and depression.[12] When someone says, "This line is too long," or "Nothing ever goes my way," or "I wish I was someplace else," the statement becomes a belief, and the emotions consistent with the belief follow. In short, complaints turn into the belief that there is something wrong with reality. This often snowballs, as one complaint brings on a wave of emotion that influences other beliefs in turn, and more negative emotions result from those beliefs. All of these unhelpful complaints stem from an overidentification with left brain and the illusory self, for it is only the ego that can object to reality as it is.

On the other side, gratitude is a reflection of the right brain. To be clear, being grateful goes beyond simple acceptance of reality into the realm of being thankful for it. For instance, if the right brain could speak, rather than saying "I accept the fact that it is raining," it might say, "I am so glad that it is raining." Research has determined there is greater activity in the right brain when subjects experienced the sensations of gratitude,[13] and another study found that subjects who were more grateful actually had more gray matter in certain parts of the right brain.[14]

In one study, subjects were randomly assigned to one of two groups. The first group regularly described five things they were grateful for, while the second group listed five things they felt were a hassle. After ten weeks, the grateful group was more optimistic about the future, had fewer health complaints, and even spent more time exercising.[15]

In many ways, gratitude reflects every opposite quality of the interpreter. We have a choice in our perspective: we can see things from a place of complaining or one of gratitude. Oliver Sacks, one of my favorite writers in neurology, was well aware of this choice. When Sacks was facing his own death, he wrote a short book called *Gratitude*.[16] In it, he wrote "I cannot pretend that I am without fear. But my predominate feeling is one of gratitude. I have loved and been loved; I have been given much and I have given something in return. Above all, I have been a sentient being, a thinking animal, on this beautiful planet, and that in itself has been an enormous privilege and adventure."

Being grateful is a choice that brings us away from the left-brain interpreter and into better alignment with the powers of the right brain.

Compassion is also an arena of the right brain. In Buddhism, compassion is often described as "the ability to see another person as potentially ourselves" or "to see the interconnectivity of all things." Compassion is all about the big picture, at which the right brain excels. I would add that true compassion only occurs when we can imagine ourselves in the position of another.

Rebecca Saxe is a cognitive neuroscientist who has spent quite a bit of time and energy exploring how the brain understands others' thoughts, and she may have found a part of the right brain that is critical in allowing us to experience compassion.[17] To make this point, consider the following scenario as an experiment:

Grace and Sally are taking a tour of a chemical plant. Grace walks over to the coffeemaker to pour some coffee. Sally asks for some too, with sugar. The white powder next to the coffee machine is a deadly chemical accidentally left behind by a scientist, but the container is clearly marked "sugar." Grace believes the white powder is sugar. She put the substance into Sally's coffee. Sally drinks it and dies.

How responsible is Grace for Sally's death? I will bet that you will not find her responsible at all, and it turns out that your right brain is critical in making this judgment. There is a section of the right brain called the right temporoparietal junction (RTPJ) that does nothing else except to think about other people's perspective. Saxe's research found that the more people can relate to the mind of Grace and understand that from her perspective she was innocent, the more active the RTPJ was. Alternately, when a magnetic pulse was applied to the RTPJ to disrupt its function, subjects were less able to consider the mind of Grace.

As it turns out, the RTPJ isn't fully developed in kids, and they have a difficult time seeing things from others' point of view until this area matures. Anyone who has spent time around young children can attest to this, as it's virtually impossible for a two- or three-year-old to relate to the needs of his or her peers when it comes to sharing a coveted toy.

Mythologist Joseph Campbell said this about compassion: "When real trouble comes, your humanity is awakened." Consider that many of us will run into a burning building to save a total stranger without a second thought, which is illogical to the left-brain interpreter. Like it or not, our true self is more compassionate than the left brain can ever admit. Bringing the left brain's desire to be master into balance allows for extraordinary compassion and interconnection with others.

Creativity

Another area that has long been associated with the right side of the brain is creativity. While there is some recent criticism of this in the neuroscience community as being overly simplistic, let's take a look quickly at why the right side of the brain has earned this distinction.

In terms of neural wiring, the left and right sides of the brain differ in physical structure. The left brain has fewer connections, both *within*—but also *to*—the rest of the brain. The right brain has more and longer fibrous connections both within itself and also to the rest of the brain.[18] This greater neural connectivity allows the right brain to make novel connections between diverse ideas, and because of this it is often labeled as the creative side of the brain.

When most people think of creativity, they focus on traditional artistic pursuits such as painting, sculpting, or writing, but the truth is that creativity applies to a much broader range of activities. For instance, here is a popular test of creativity that measures one's ability to make connections between things that seem, well, remote and distant.[19]

What is one word that connects the following three words:

Widow

Bite

Monkey

If the word *spider* just popped into your mind, it is likely with the help of your right brain. This association is creative because the connections are not immediately obvious.

In this way creativity could be described as a form of intelligence in and of itself, one that has been instrumental in discoveries often associated with the left brain. For instance, Albert Einstein is one of the best-known scientists of all time, a master of a field that is based on logic and rational thinking. However, he was able to perceive the connection between moving in space and the slowing of time in a novel way that wasn't apparent to anyone else.

Furthermore, many artists feel that their creativity is linked to their intuition. Author Ray Bradbury once said, "Your intuition knows what to write, so get out of the way."[20] Filmmaker and artist David Lynch goes even further, saying that "Intuition is the key to everything, in painting, filmmaking, business—everything. I think you could have an intellectual ability, but if you can sharpen your intuition . . . a knowingness occurs."[21] Beyond artists, there are many other notable examples of people who attribute some of their greatest successes to the power of their intuition, such as Steve Jobs, Oprah Winfrey, and Carl Jung.

In the areas of intuition, emotion, and creativity, right-brain intelligence brings "wisdom beyond words." Even as the left-brain interpreter ignores or minimizes what goes on in its counterpart, it's impossible to deny the power and potency of the right brain—which provides life-changing insights, bursts of intuitive genius, and leaps of creative problem-solving.

Explorations
A Day without Complaining

In my classes, I challenge students to see how long they can go without complaining and then ask them to write about the results. I define complaining as finding some fault with reality, so again, simply being skeptical about something or offering a helpful critique doesn't count. This project has resulted in some of the most insightful student papers I have read in my career. I've had dozens of students point out what a surprise it was that complaining had become so habitual that they didn't even know it was going on. I've also had students tell me they "love" to complain and had not thought of changing things, which is also a powerful insight. Many students admitted that they could not even make it to the end of class without some sort of complaint.

While some students do believe they love to complain, more often I find that students become aware of more negative feelings after a long complaint session. Rather than feeling good or getting relief from letting off steam though long, drawn-out complaining with friends, most said they usually felt worse.

Intuition Test

We've spent quite a bit of time on the underappreciated powers of the right brain, but it is by no means infallible. One of the most important questions for modern psychology is finding out when we should trust our intuition and when the left brain might rightly signal us to keep it in check or override it. In the 1970s, psychology spent some time showing us that our gut instincts can actually get us into trouble.[22] Let me give one example:

I will only tell you four things about Jim. Jim is short, thin, wears glasses, and likes to read poetry. Is Jim more likely:

A. An Ivy League English professor

or

B. A truck driver?

Where did your intuitive feelings guide you on this one? Did *A* just pop into your mind? Let's think about this—by which I mean apply some more rigorous linear reasoning. How many Ivy League English professors exist in the world? How many are short? Thin? Wear glasses? Like to read poetry? Okay . . . Now how many truck drivers are there worldwide? Even without knowing the exact numbers, there are obviously far more truck drivers, and therefore the true probability is far greater that Jim is a truck driver.

Here's another example. Imagine you are at the roulette wheel and it has come up red for the last five spins. Where do you put your money for the next spin? Red or black? The gambler's fallacy is when people believe they should shift to black, because after so many red spins it feels like it is now more probable that the next one will be black. However, in reality, each spin is unaffected by the previous ones. Numerous other examples have shown that when we use our "gut," we are prone to stereotypes, overgeneralizations, and guesswork that can really take us down a bad path.

So while intuition is documentable and real, it is also something we can't produce at will, and as the truck driver and gambler examples show, we have to be careful not to rely on it erroneously. Perhaps particularly in the West where the left-brain interpreter "master" does not honor the gift of the intuitive mind, very few people learn to develop this form of knowing or put systems in place to guard against its pitfalls.

Call on Intuition for a Big Decision

Have a big decision to make? One study suggests that when making major purchases (in this study participants were purchasing automobiles), those who did so based on an intuitive nudge or gut feeling were ultimately happier with the outcome than those who spent a long time deliberating.[23] The next time you have a major decision to make, take note of your initial gut feeling regarding it, as this study suggests you should likely follow it. Your right brain might have big-picture information of which you (i.e., the left brain interpreter) are not fully conscious that will affect the outcome of your choice.

SEVEN

What Is Consciousness?

For the one who perceives all beings as the Self,
there will be no more delusion or grief.
—The Upanishads

So far in this book, we have looked at evidence from neu-ropsychology that supports important ideas of Buddhism and other Eastern philosophical traditions, namely that the self we all take for granted is in fact an illusion and that this illusion is the cause of much, if not all, of the mental suffering we experience as humans. This can be difficult to consider, especially because the left-brain interpreter is not only convincing in its illusionary nature, but also working feverishly to prevent its fiction from being realized.

We have also spent some time looking at the right side of the brain and found that even though it is silent in terms of verbal thought and is therefore labeled "unconscious" by the left-brain interpreter, it has an intelligence all its own. Furthermore, in the areas of finding meaning and understanding the whole, it is the "conscious" left brain that must rely on the "unconscious" right.

Whether or not you're convinced by this evidence, I do think there is one thing we can all agree on, and that is the fact that we are conscious. In other words, humans share what we could call a sense of perception that none of us can deny. Because our sense of self feels so central to our consciousness, what would it mean for consciousness if the self were indeed a fiction?

As a matter of background, contemporary neuroscience has one belief above and beyond all others, and that is that consciousness is localized in the brain. Because of this brain-specific localization, traditional neuroscience assumes that consciousness itself is also individual—that is, it exists separately in separate brains. In other words, I have "my consciousness" and you have yours, and in this sense the interpretive mind thinks and acts as if it "owns" consciousness.

While the brain and consciousness are clearly connected—if you shook my head long enough, I would become dizzy—this may not tell the whole story. After all, the world isn't flat simply because it appears so in Kansas.

Consider the work of author and researcher Rupert Sheldrake, who is taking science to task by questioning many of its unnecessary assumptions, one of which is that consciousness is locked up in the skull. Sheldrake believes that consciousness can extend beyond the skull and is more akin to what he calls a *morphic field*.[1] For those of you unfamiliar with the term, in the scientific world a *field* refers to a kind of invisible force that does not have the same properties or act the same way that material objects do. *Morphic fields* stick to or surround a material object. For instance, think of how a magnetic field extends beyond the magnet itself. You can cut up the magnet into as many pieces as you like, but the magnetic field is still preserved because the field itself is holistic and cannot be dissected.

Animals, which lack the developed left-brain interpreter of humans, may offer some evidence that consciousness extends outside the brain.[2] Sheldrake points out that cats often know (and dread) when it is time to go the vet and will hide from their owner. Of course, owners will counter with strategies that minimize cues that it is time to go to the vet, but the cats still seem to know. Of the sixty-five pet clinics he contacted, sixty-four stated that it is extremely common for cat owners to miss their appointments because the owner couldn't find the cat. In the sixty-fifth clinic, it was so common they gave up the practice of having appointments altogether.

Pet owners will often attest that their pets seem to know when a member of the family is coming home or when someone is about to come to the front door. In my own case, we have a five-pound neurotic dog in our house, and my wife is the center of his universe. For years, I noticed that our dog always seemed to know when my wife was coming home and he would start to run in circles, run to the window, then run in circles again. What caught my attention is when he would do this at times when there were no cues that she was coming home. That is, her arrival was unexpected, e.g., she forgot something and had to turn around, and our dog would know before I did.

However, to be valid science, one has to make sure we are not just remembering the hits and forgetting the misses. Sheldrake conducted a careful study on such occurrences where pet owners would randomly get a call to head home.[3] The owners would then head home in a taxi making sure that there were no other cues that they were on their way. What he found was that the animals began to act excited at the exact point when the intentions of the owner were to head home. This suggests some sort of connection between the consciousness of the pet and its owner.

In a final anecdote from the animal world, a chicken became known as "Miracle Mike" in the mid twentieth century after it survived an attempted beheading on the chopping block. Although the only thing left above the neck was the brain stem and one ear, the chicken was kept alive by his owner who, seeing his resiliency, decided to spare the chicken and put food and water directly into his neck via an eyedropper. Mike lived for another two years with no head, otherwise walked and behaved normally, and even toured with a circus. In Mike's case, it would seem impossible to argue that its consciousness was in the brain.

If we allow for a moment the idea that consciousness does extend beyond the brain, it might also explain some of the phenomena currently called psychic or paranormal. (Notice if your left brain has a dismissive reaction to these terms, which is common in the scientific community.) One example of such phenomena is what Stanford researchers Russell Targ and Harold Puthoff called remote viewing, or the ability to see, in the "mind's eye" only, distant targets and locations. A program to study and develop remote-viewing techniques was actually funded by the U.S. government's Central Intelligence Agency in the 1970s and 1980s.[4]

Remote viewing is just a fancy term for what parapsychology calls *clairvoyance* (the word itself comes from the French terms for "clear" and "vision") and refers to the ability to gain information about a person, object, or event via a form of extrasensory perception. Being able to sense something that lies beyond the reach of your physical senses might well mean that your consciousness also goes to this distant place.

If we take examples of psychic ability as having a kernel of truth, then I think it suggests consciousness does extend, at least for some people and in some instances, outside of the brain. Furthermore, perhaps intuition can also be explained in part by the idea that consciousness extends outside the brain.

While these ideas are speculative, there is one thing I can confirm without a doubt, and that is that in spite of the best efforts and best technologies modern science has to offer, the neuroscience community has not located consciousness in the brain. Perhaps the simple reason for this is that consciousness is not there to be found. What if the brain is connected to, or a part of, consciousness—rather than a possessor of consciousness.

If consciousness arises from the brain simply tapping into a larger field of consciousness, rather than existing as an object within the brain, then like our sense of self, it begins to look and feel more like a verb than a noun. Nouns are solid and immobile, while verbs are fluid and active. Verbs move across space and time and are difficult to localize.

Perhaps every morning, consciousness tunes in to seven billion brains. After waking, this consciousness would have access to particular memories and seven billion unique perspectives (each its own "pilot") and the interpreter would be reborn. Perhaps this is exactly what happened this morning. Perhaps consciousness would identify as that unique person and never suspect it wasn't that person, just like you think you are you right now. If this is the case, then perhaps the idea of consciousness as an "observer," which is often mentioned in spiritual circles, should be understood more accurately as simply an "observance."

If this were true, it would upend our most fundamental belief. Of all the ideas that we have discussed, the idea that consciousness sits behind the eyes and between the ears feels rock-solid for most of us. This experience is tied directly to the illusion of an inner self. These ideas work together, and the result is that it feels like there is a "me" from inside the skull. I hope you are beginning to consider that both of these ideas—individual consciousness and the self—might well be illusions.

As a final note on consciousness, modern science rests on the assumption that material things like brains are primary. By this I mean that scientists think that a brain and only a brain can give rise to consciousness. But here again, is it possible that the opposite is true? Is consciousness giving rise to matter? This is what so many Eastern philosophical schools tell us, and if they are right about the nonexistence of the self, is it possible they are right about this too? Advaita Vedanta teacher Nisargadatta Maharaj said, "You are not in the world, but the world is in you. It is only a result of consciousness." This idea begins to sound a whole lot like the Heart Sutra again, where emptiness (space) gives rise to form (matter). While a full discussion of this topic is beyond the scope of this book, it does leave us with something to ponder.

Explorations
Consciousness Misdirected
The next two exercises show how easy it is to shift the relationship between consciousness and the body, suggesting that consciousness is more pliable and less rooted in the brain than we might think.

The first is simple enough to set up in my classroom. I ask two students to sit in chairs, one right behind the other, with both students facing the same direction. Student A is in the back, facing Student B's back. I then have both students either close their eyes or don a blindfold. As the experimenter, I take Student A's right hand with my right and guide their index finger to tap the nose of Student B, who is seated in front of them. At the same time, I also use my left hand to tap on student A's nose. I control the tapping so that they are in perfect synchrony.

Consider the message being sent to Student A's brain: my hand is two feet in front of me touching a nose. Incredibly, and without fail, Student A's brain then makes a radical revision based on the physical evidence; it assumes *its own real nose is two feet long*. Afterward, Student A sometimes reports that they felt their nose slowly grow two feet, and sometimes it seems to have grown instantly. The experience is often so profound and surprising that, even in a roomful of others, Student A will let out a scream.

There is another form of this illusion I've used in the lab; you need a fake rubber hand (you can easily procure these at Halloween stores), a table, and a large piece of cardboard.[5] The subject sits at a table and puts their hand out such that the cardboard is upright and they can't see their hand. The fake hand is put right in front of them, resting in a way that their own hand might naturally. Now, the experimenter asks them to look at the fake hand while they give a series of taps and short strokes to both the fake hand and the subject's real hand, randomly and in perfect synchrony. Again, imagine the messages in the brain of the subject: I'm looking at a fake rubber hand that is being tapped exactly the same time as my own hand. Then the subject's brain makes a radical revision: the fake hand is actually mine. The subject actually relocates consciousness into the fake rubber hand.

Once the illusion is felt, the experimenter can do anything from smash the fake hand with a hammer to injecting it with a long needle. In past experiments, the reaction to this was just as if the subject had experienced the real pain of having their real hand smashed or stuck with a needle.

Dr. V. S. Ramachandran, the neuroscientist mentioned earlier in the book, has created an interesting treatment for people experiencing the sensation of phantom limbs.[6] People who have lost a limb sometimes have the strange sensation that the limb is still there. In the worst circumstance the phantom limb is experiencing pain. In one example, the patient's phantom hand had such a tightly closed fist that the phantom nails were digging into the hand, causing extreme distress. But how can medical science deal with pain in a limb that doesn't even exist? Ramachandran believed that by tricking the patient's brain he could bring some relief. He set up a box with mirrors such that when the patient put their attached hand into an opening, mirrors made it look like the patient actually had two hands—the missing hand was supplanted by a reflection of the remaining hand. The patient put in his existing hand and opened a closed fist. All the brain—or perhaps consciousness—needed to see was the phantom hand open up its clenched fist, and the pain was gone.

Test Your Psychic Abilities

This exploration is a fun way to test the idea for yourself that consciousness may extend outside the skull. You'll need a deck of cards, a quiet room, and four or more friends to join you. To begin, take five cards at random from the deck and place them faceup on a table. Next, choose one person who will be the "receiver," and ask them to leave the room for a moment. The remaining members of the group, the "senders," pick one of the five cards as the choice card. Invite the receiver back into the room and don't share which card the group has chosen.

Ask all of the senders to be silent and make no eye contact with the receiver as the receiver holds his or her hand over each card to see if the correct card can be "felt." Here's the last step. When the receiver has their hand over the wrong card, every member of the sender group should say the word *no* silently in their minds only, as if they were sending the receiver a message.

When the receiver has a hand over the correct card, the senders should say the word *yes* in their mind only, to let the receiver know that is the card the group selected. The receiver shouldn't be rushed and is looking for a subtle difference in feeling over each card. Finally the receiver will make a selection. Statistically, if this is all meaningless, the choice will be right 20 percent of the time given there are five cards. I have a friend who does this with groups regularly, and he says the percentages are almost always higher than that, with some groups guessing correctly 80 percent of the time. While this is hardly a scientific study, it is a fun way to test this ability for yourself.[7]

EIGHT

Finding the Real You

Everything will come all right for you in the end.
—Ramana Maharishi

Every semester, at least one student will ask me, sometimes in clear distress, "If my left-brain interpreter is a fiction, who is the *real* me?" I'll make an attempt to answer that question, as I do for them, but before I do, I want to remind you that this is *always* what the left-brain interpreter asks. That's because the interpreter loves conclusion, certainty, and has a constant need to "think about it all," and this question is an example of the very process that creates and sustains the fiction it has established.

Turning to the right brain, perhaps it already knows the answer or it doesn't much care. Another possibility is that the real you—whoever that is—loves a mystery. Either way, I will do my best to respond to this question using a method that will appeal to both sides of the brain: a simple story.

In the East there is a classic tale about hide-and-seek told by various masters, but they all go something like this: In the beginning there was only God, so God had no one to play with except God. Therefore, God created a game of hide-and-seek, but the only way he could do this was to pretend that he was who he wasn't and that he wasn't who he was. In other words, God could only play this game by forgetting himself. God got lost in each of us and in all of our drama in order to experience adventure, even if this sometimes turns out terribly. Even the worst suffering is like a bad dream, and it is all over when God wakes up.

Imagine that you were an all-powerful and all-knowing entity and your existence is only eternal bliss. Would you choose this existence if you could? What if the only way to make things interesting would be to hide from what you are, or to be exactly what you are not, in a game of pretend? Suddenly the game would be "afoot," and there would be great drama and excitement in finding yourself. Of course, you could never know this was a game, or it wouldn't work.

Would you want to watch a movie without conflict, a villain, and a challenge to overcome, featuring characters that have no goal and nothing to achieve? In this movie, things are fine just as they are. The actors just sit in meditative bliss, or go for walks in nature, or hold hands, all while we watch. It is difficult to imagine such a movie and more so to think you might enjoy it. Even with the best actors and special effects, it would likely be a record-setting flop.

How much fun would it be to gamble in a casino that you owned? There would be no way to really *win* because if you did win, you would lose and if you lost, you'd still win. The only way to have fun in your own casino is to forget that you are the owner. Only then would the wins be a rush and the losses seem tragic, even if neither was really the case.

While it may sound strange to suggest that this is what's happening to us, I think—or rather, I feel—that this story points to the true nature of our existence. Perhaps an all-powerful eternal force would do exactly what is happening right now, hiding from itself in billions of ways, within you right now reading this sentence, unaware of its essence and at the same time realizing everything is in perfect harmony.

All play, all adventure, requires a challenge that must be overcome or an evil force that must be fought against and destroyed. The Christians call this evil or sin, the Buddhists call it the three poisons (fear, greed, and delusion), the Freudians call it the id, and Jung called it the shadow, but it's the same mechanism woven into the fabric of a universe intent on play and an unending mystery.

The issue with any game—even this grand universe game—is that unless there is a possibility of defeat—and it has to be "real" defeat—there is no game. The grand game of all games is the game of life and death. If death didn't seem real, the game would be meaningless. Death seems like a real, genuine defeat because if it didn't, we would lose interest in the game.

I remember when my son was young and I would chase him, pretending that I was a monster. He would yell over and over again, laughing, "A monster is going to get me!" Likewise, I would hold him, leaning back as he almost fell off my lap, and we would play the game of "Don't let me go," with both of us laughing over and over and each time I would extend him a little farther and make the game a little more exciting. This is the early form of drama without the seriousness we give it later in life when we forget that the original nature of drama is to play.

As adults, our monsters become very real—taking such forms such as financial ruin, loneliness, job loss, sickness, and death. As adults we've come to really believe that monsters can "get us" and that we will be devastated by this. Somehow a game that started with a built-in safety valve and the inability to stop laughing ends up in stress, depression, and anxiety. Not coincidentally, as our bodies get older, our sense of self becomes more established, and our propensity to experience mental suffering grows too.

Next, consider this. What if the way to "win" the game of life is to discover *experientially* that it's all a game in the first place and that you are the creator of the game? I emphasize the *experience* of this discovery, and I suggest that this is what happened to the Buddha, Lao-tzu, and other ancient masters from the East so long ago. In their case, identification with the self collapsed, and so did all the mental suffering that went with it.

If mental suffering has any benefit, perhaps it is to help you wake up to the game, to the grand drama that is this existence. As it is put in Buddhism, "when there is no mud, there is no lotus flower." The Buddha was supposedly protected from suffering early in life, and if he had never ventured out to explore suffering, he would have never had his insights. If not for your suffering, you would not be where you are right now.

Let's conclude with a few explicit pointers on playing this cosmic game.

One way to play the game is to dismiss or forget the ideas presented here and continue to believe that the left brain is in fact you. You keep your identity and keep playing a role in this theatrical world we call modern society. In this realm of categories and interpretations, there are good days, but there are also bad days; there are friends, but also enemies. In this left-brain world, you can win, but sometimes you will lose. There is the thrill of victory but also the anxiety over defeat. The game is played with a dreadful sense of seriousness and urgency, as if it isn't a game at all.

Of course, there are some downsides in this approach. Life is viewed as short. Death and disease are the enemy, and you must work as hard as you can for as long as possible, trying to win with the most possible credits, be they material or spiritual. Like most of us, your actor ego is likely cast as only an extra in the background of the world's stage, but there is always the chance for stardom, and for that chance, many accept the suffering. There is nothing wrong with this choice, and currently and historically it is the most popular option on the planet. In a way, for those who are totally ignorant of all these ideas, we could say that they are playing the game so well that their left brains should be congratulated.

Going to the other extreme, another option would be to wholeheartedly pursue activities associated with the right side of the brain, in a search for what many refer to as enlightenment. Taking this option to the fullest means following a path similar to the saints, masters, and monks of the world's great spiritual traditions, and of course, the Buddha. Meditation, mindfulness, prayer, yoga, and maintaining a focus on compassion, gratitude, and the interconnected nature of all existence are all great places to start. Ultimately how to "get there" is largely a mystery and certainly something that cannot be articulated fully in words, but there are many signs and pointers the adepts have left behind. If this is your calling, then I bow to you and wish you well in your journey.

A third option is what one might call a middle path, where you have one foot in each of the other two options. In this option, you take the game just seriously enough that you cheer when your kid wins a soccer game and feel sad when you don't get a promotion at work. Of course in either case, you don't take either the victory or defeat too seriously, because behind them both you maintain a hint of a smile and this smile symbolizes your understanding that without losing there can be no winning and that every win ultimately depends on a loss.

In this middle path, you might look at a trashy magazine in the grocery store and simultaneously see it as gossipy nonsense and an expression of human creativity and spirituality. You might feel a surge of anger when someone cuts you off in traffic, while at the same time be laughing internally at the silliness of the drama. There may be moments when you experience the egoless consciousness and the total embrace of "no self, no problem," but then a few minutes later your ego kicks in when a coworker walks by and ignores you.

In fact, you may already be playing the game in exactly this way. Maybe you meditate, practice mindfulness, and feel very spiritually grounded when you do, and later the ego comes back online and is frustrated to find out that you've run out of coffee. You take a yoga class and feel great, but curse the person that left a scratch on your car when you leave to go home. To become aware of these machinations of the mind without becoming attached to them is a kind of modern middle path.

No matter your choice in how to play, my hope is that by reading this book and becoming familiar with the left-brain interpreter and how it works, you can start to take it a little less seriously. Doing so will most certainly lessen your suffering.

You may even stop trying so hard to change certain things in your life, or to become this or that in the future, because you begin to notice that the problems you are trying to overcome are mostly creations of the left-brain interpreter and you see how once they are overcome the left-brain interpreter will simply create new ones. This can also be true even for those pursuing a strict spiritual path, as indicated by the words of former Harvard professor Richard Alpert (now known as Ram Dass) when he said, "All spiritual practices are illusions created by illusionists to escape illusion."

On this middle path, on one foot you consider that the real you is already perfect and at peace, and that's good because the left-brain interpreter has no real power to create change in your life anyway, because it's a mirage—though I'll bet your left-brain interpreter is objecting to this right now. Think of it this way, can the smoke above a factory do anything to change the workings of the factory itself? How frustrating would it be to believe that the fictional character Sherlock Holmes could solve a mystery in the real world? When we get this, we begin to see that we are right where we need to be, doing exactly what we need to be doing.

So while several explorations have been offered in this book to help "you" get out of your left brain, perhaps the *real* you already is, and it's not worried one bit. This is the type of paradox that frustrates the interpreter, but to experience this is to experience the playful nature of reality, which takes us back to the story of God playing hide-and-seek.

People enjoy a scary movie or an amusement park ride *because* they know that they are actually safe. In this same sense, this universal consciousness knows everything is safe, even in what the left brain categorizes as horrific tragedies. If you were an all-powerful, all-knowing consciousness, you could never know sadness, loss, anxiety, surprise, or the excitement of not knowing what will happen next. An all-knowing consciousness could not enjoy jokes or cry at tragedies. By playing the game, consciousness delights in every experience possible, and the only way to do that is for it to lose itself in us. If you want to have an infinite set of experiences, create fictitious egos that take themselves seriously and program them to always desire what they do not have.

In the same way that a glass of water is exponentially more satisfying after a five-mile hike in the desert, the experience of feeling the interconnectedness of everything is more fulfilling after the illusion of separation. This is the fun of the game. This is the fun of waking up.

This game is a privilege and an adventure, but it is also sometimes a comedy and sometimes a tragedy. The whole of it makes up a tapestry such that you cannot selectively pull one part out and leave the others behind because they are all interwoven, defining each other, and even giving existence to each other. Perhaps the real you knows this perfectly, because it wove the tapestry together in the first place. If this book has served its purpose, it has been a reminder that there is no place to go and nothing in particular to do, because you are already there and already doing it. Except of course that there isn't even a real you anywhere, doing anything. Or, perhaps we could say it is also everywhere and doing everything.

That might make an excellent koan on which to meditate.

Exploration
Who Am I?

In a variety of spiritual traditions, one of the most powerful questions to ask oneself is *who am I?* Rather than answer with the left-brain interpreter via descriptive labels, comparison, categories, or pattern perception, try and turn your mind inward to see if you can find the source of the "I" thought. You could do this in a meditation setting, but it need not be reserved for such a time, as you can really try this at any time during the day, even if just for a few seconds. As you do this, consider that the answer to the question may be a feeling rather than a thought, one that is found in the space and the silence that is all around us.

Other related questions to ponder as you undertake this exploration are as follows:

- Am I the name someone gave to me?

- Am I the gender that was assigned to me?

- Am I the job that I work at?

- Am I the social roles that I play?

- Am I the age society tells me I am?

- Am I the intelligence society defines me as?

- Am I my level of education?

- Am I the body that others define me as?

- Am I the thoughts in my head?

- Am I the memories that I think happened?

- Am I my preferences? That is, the things I like?

- Am I my desires?

- Am I my emotions?

- Am I my beliefs?

- Am I my reactions?

- Am I my expectations?

- Am I the movies that play in my mind?

- Am I a mystery?

The *real* you cannot be put into words . . . categories, labels, beliefs, emotions, or anything that can be labeled as "known."

Notes and References

All references and quotes from the Buddha are from these two sources, unless stated otherwise: *The Dhammapada: The Saying of the Buddha* (1976). Translated by Thomas Byrom. New York, Knopf; "Anatta-lakkhana Sutta: The Discourse on the Not-self Characteristic" (SN 22.59), translated from the Pali by N.K.G. Mendis. *Access to Insight (BCBS Edition)*, 13 June 2010, http://www.accesstoinsight.org/tipitaka/sn/sn22/sn22.059.mend.html.

Preface

1. One of the first popular books connecting Eastern philosophy and physics was Capra, F. (1975). *The Tao of Physics: An Exploration of the Parallels Between Modern Physics and Eastern Mysticism*. Berkeley: Shambhala.

2. Houshmand, Z., Wallace, B., and Livingston, R. (1999). *Consciousness at the Crossroads: Conversations with the Dalai Lama on Brain Science and Buddhism*. Snow Lion. Ithaca, NY. This book resulted from meetings of the Dalai Lama and a group of eminent neuroscientists and psychiatrists.

3. Kaul, P., Passafiume, J., Sargent, C. R., and O'Hara, B. F. (2010). "Meditation acutely improves psychomotor vigilance, and may decrease sleep need." *Behavioral and Brain Functions* 6: 47.

4. For Sara Lazar's talk about changing the brain with meditation, see "How Meditation Can Reshape Our Brains: Sara Lazar at TEDxCambridge 2011." https://youtu.be /m8rRzTtP7Tc.

A more detailed article reviewing her work would be Lazar, S. (2013). "The neurobiology of mindfulness." *Mindfulness and Psychotherapy*, 282–294. Two works about meditation, compassion, and reducing the amygdala are Hölzel, B., Carmody, J., Evans, K., Hoge, E., Dusek, J., Morgan, L., Pitman, R., and Lazar, S. (2010). "Stress reduction correlates with structural changes in the amygdala." *Social Cognitive and Affective Neuroscience* Vol. 5, Issue 1 (1 March 2010): 11–17; Hölzel, B. K., Carmody, J., Vangel, M., Congleton, C., Yerramsetti, S. M., Gard, T., and Lazar, S. W. (2011). "Mindfulness practice leads to increases in regional brain gray matter density." *Psychiatry Research* 191(1): 36–43. http://doi .org/10.1016/j.pscychresns.2010.08.006.

5. Research on tai chi has become so extensive that there is now a review article that examines the numerous other scientific reviews (107 reviews in total) on the subject: Solloway, M. R., Taylor, S. L., Shekelle, P. G., Miake-Lye, I. M., Beroes, J. M., Shanman, R. M., and Hempel, S. (2016). "An evidence map of the effect of Tai Chi on health outcomes." *Systematic Reviews* 5(1).

6. Büssing, A., Michalsen, A., Khalsa, S. B. S., Telles, S., and Sherman, K. J. (2012). "Effects of yoga on mental and

physical health: A short summary of reviews." *Evidence-Based Complementary and Alternative Medicine: eCAM*, 165410. http://doi.org/10.1155/2012/165410.

7. Villemure, C., Čeko, M., Cotton, V. A., and Bushnell, M. C. (2015). "Neuroprotective effects of yoga practice: Age-, experience-, and frequency-dependent plasticity." *Frontiers in Human Neuroscience* 9: 281. http://doi.org/10.3389/fnhum.2015.00281.

8. Creswell, J. D. (2015) "Biological pathways linking mindfulness with health." Eds. Brown, K. W., Creswell J. D., and Ryan, R. *Handbook on Mindfulness Science*. Guilford Publications, New York, NY; Creswell, J. D., Taren, A., Lindsay, E., Greco, C., Gianaros, P., Fairgrieve, A., Marsland, A., Brown, K., Way, B., Rosen, R., and Ferris, J. (2016). "Alterations in resting state functional connectivity link mindfulness meditation with reduced interleukin-6: a randomized controlled trial." *Biological Psychiatry*; DOI: 10.1016/j.biopsych.2016.01.008.

Introduction

1. Morin, A. (2010). "Self-recognition, theory-of-mind, and self-awareness: What side are you on?" *Laterality,* 16(3): 367–383.

2. Wei, W. W. (1963). *Ask the Awakened: the Negative Way.* Sentient Publications.

3. As the neuroscientist Tim Crow put it, "Except in the light of brain hemisphere lateralization, nothing in human psychology makes any sense." In other words, the only way to understand who we truly are is to examine the left and right sides of the brain.

Chapter 1: Meet the Interpreter—
An Accidental Discovery

1. Works explaining the left-brain interpreter and its discovery include Gazzaniga, M. S., and LeDoux, J. E. (1978). *The Integrated Mind.* New York: Plenum Press; Gazzaniga, M.S. (1985). *The Social Brain: Discovering the Networks of the Mind.* New York: Basic Books; Gazzaniga, M. S. (1998, July). "The split brain revisited." *Scientific American* 279(1): 35–39.

2. Nisbett and Wilson (1977). "Telling more than we can know: Verbal reports on mental processes." *Psychological Review* 84: 231–259; Johansson, P., Hall, L., Sikström, S., Tärning, B., and Lind, A. (2006). "How something can be said about telling more than we can know." *Consciousness and Cognition* 15(4): 673–692.

3. Dutton, D. G., and Aaron, A. P. (1974). "Some evidence for heightened sexual attraction under conditions of high anxiety." *Journal of Personality and Social Psychology* 30(4): 510–517. doi:10.1037/h0037031.

4. Dienstbier, R. (1979). "Attraction increases and decreases as a function of emotion-attribution and appropriate social cues." *Motivation and Emotion* 3: 201–218.

5. Meston, C., and Frohlich, P. (2003). "Love at first fright: Partner salience moderates roller-coaster-induced excitation transfer." *Archives of Sexual Behavior* 32(6): 537–544.

6. Gazzaniga, M. S. (1985). *The Social Brain: Discovering the Networks of the Mind.* New York: Basic Books.

Chapter 2: Language and Categories—
The Tools of the Interpreting Mind

1. Konnikova, M. (2013). "The man who couldn't speak and how he revolutionized psychology." Retrieved from https:// blogs.scientificamerican.com/literally-psyched/the-man -who-couldnt-speakand-how-he-revolutionized-psychology/.

2. To quote laterality expert Joe Hellige, "Left-hemisphere dominance for many aspects of language is the most obvious and most often cited cognitive asymmetry. In particular, the left hemisphere seems dominant for the production of overt speech . . ." (Hellige, J. B. (1993). *Hemispheric Asymmetry: What's Right and What's Left.* Cambridge, MA: Harvard University Press). However, this does not mean that the right brain does not play a role in language. To use a business metaphor, the CEO of language is in the left brain, even if it may still have some important employees working in the right brain. For example, the right brain contributes to the emotional aspects of language, and those with damage to the right brain are often emotionally flat when it comes to communicating via speech. Right brain damaged subjects may also have a difficult time with sarcasm and metaphor because these functions of language exist in an emotional realm outside of language and speech itself.

3. Morin, A. (2011). "Self-awareness, Part 2: Neuroanatomy and importance of inner speech." *Social and Personality Psychology Compass* 2(12): 1004–1012.

4. McGilchrist, I. (2009). *The Master and His Emissary: The Divided Brain and the Making of the Western World.* Yale University Press. The TED Talk by McGilchrist is available here: https://www.ted.com/talks/iain_mcgilchrist_the_divided_brain.

5. Korzybski, A. (1933). *Science and Sanity: An Introduction to Non-Aristotelian Systems and General Semantics.* Institute of General Semantics, 747–761.

6. Stroop, J. (1935). "Studies of interference in serial verbal reactions." *Journal of Experimental Psychology* 18(6): 643–662. doi:10.1037/h0054651.

7. Steve Christman, my mentor in grad school, did an interesting study on the Stroop effect. He assumed that the left brain processed the symbol of the color (the word) and the right brain processed the actual color. He found that those with the least communication between the two sides of the brain had the smallest interference when the symbol and actual color didn't match. That is, if the two sides of the brain are acting more independently, the left-brain symbol doesn't interfere with the right brain color when they differ. However, the point is that the Stroop effect shows that the left brain treats the word *YELLOW* the same as if the actual color yellow was present. Christman, S. (2001). "Individual differences in stroop and local-global processing: A possible role of interhemispheric interaction." *Brain and Cognition* 45: 97–118. 10.1006/brcg.2000.1259.

8. Teicher, M., Anderson, S., Polcari, A., Anderson, C., Navalta, C., and Kim, D. (2003). "The neurobiological consequences of early stress and childhood maltreatment." *Neuroscience and Biobehavioral Reviews* 27: 33–44. The only way this could happen is if we are treating words as if they *are* the things they represent.

9. Salzen, E. A. (1998). "Emotion and self-awareness." *Applied Animal Behaviour Science* 57: 299–313.

10. Loftus, E. F., and Palmer, J. C. (1974). "Reconstruction of auto-mobile destruction: An example of the interaction between language and memory." *Journal of Verbal Learning and Verbal Behavior* 13: 585–589.

11. *Placebo* means "I shall please" and refers to when a subject's belief in a particular outcome in a study creates that particular outcome. Although the placebo effect can be traced back a few hundred years in medicine, it wasn't until the 1950s that the term "placebo effect" was used in a research paper: Beecher, H. K. (1955). "The powerful placebo." *JAMA* 1955; 159(17):1602–1606. doi:10.1001/jama.1955.02960340022006.

12. Recent research has questioned if the widespread use and effectiveness of antidepressants are not largely due to the placebo effect. See Kirsch, I. (2008). "Challenging received wisdom: Antidepressants and the placebo effect." *McGill Journal of Medicine : MJM* 11(2): 219–222.

13. Benedetti, Fabrizio, Carlino, Elisa, and Pollo, Antonella (2011). "How placebos change the patient's brain." *Neuropsychopharmacology: Official Publication of the American College of Neuropsychopharmacology* 36: 339–354. 10.1038/npp.2010.81.

14. Alia-Klein, N., Goldstein, R. Z., Tomasi, D., Zhang, L., Fagin-Jones, S., Telang, F., Wang, G. J., Fowler, J. S., and Volkow, N. D. (2007). "What is in a Word? *No* versus *yes* differentially engage the lateral orbitofrontal cortex." *Emotion (Washington, D.C.)* 7(3): 649–659. http://doi.org/10.1037/1528-3542.7.3.649.

15. One classic work on koans is Hori, V. (2003). *Zen Sand: The Book of Capping Phrases for Kōan Practice*. University of Hawaii Press.

Chapter 3: Pattern Perception and the Missing Self

1. This isn't to say the right brain is not able to recognize patterns. In fact, even the early split-brain research demonstrated that if the word *spoon* was flashed to the right brain, it would pick out and recognize a spoon using the left hand. It is more a matter of degree. Think of the left brain as the Johann Sebastian Bach of pattern recognition, whereas the right brain is more of the garage band of pattern recognition. However, this imbalance plays an important role in this journey we call the human experience. It may even define what is unique about the human experience.

2. Taylor, I., and Taylor, M. M. (1990). *Psycholinguistics: Learning and Using Language*. Pearson, 367; Gebauer, D., Fink, A., Kargl, R., Reishofer, G., Koschutnig, K., Purgstaller, C., et al. (2012). "Differences in brain function and changes with intervention in children with poor spelling and reading abilities." *PLoS ONE* 7(5): e38201. https://doi.org/10.1371/journal.pone.0038201

3. Booth, J. R., and Burman, D. D. (2001). "Development and disorders of neurocognitive systems for oral language and reading." *Learning Disability Quarterly* 24: 205–215.

4 . Rorschach, H. (1924). *Manual for Rorschach Ink-blot Test*. Chicago: Stoelting.

5. Wolford, G., Miller, M. B., and Gazzaniga, M. (2000). "The left hemisphere's role in hypothesis formation." *The Journal of Neuroscience* 20.

6. Tucker, D. M., and Williamson, P. A. (1984). "Asymmetric neural control systems in human self-regulation." *Psychological Review*. 91: 185–215.

7. Krummenacher, P., Mohr, C., Haker, H., and Brugger, P. (2010). "Dopamine, paranormal belief, and the detection of meaningful stimuli." *Journal of Cognitive Neuroscience* 22: 1670–1681. It should be very interesting to the reader that the left side of the brain not only excels at seeing things that are not there but it also creates the image of the self or ego.

8. Whitson, J., and Galinsky, A. (2008). "Seeing patterns when there is nothing to see." *Science*: 115–117. doi : 10.1126/science.1159845.

9. Simonov, P. V., Frolov, M. V., Evtushenko, V. F., and Sviridov, E. P. (1977). "Effect of emotional stress on recognition of visual patterns." *Aviation, Space, and Environmental Medicine* 48: 856–858.

10. Proulx, T., and Heine, S. J. (2010). "The frog in Kierkegaard's beer: Finding meaning in the threat-compensation literature." *Social and Personality Psychology Compass* 4(10): 889–905. http://dx.doi.org/10.1111/j.1751 -9004.2010.00304.x.

Chapter 4: The Basics of Right-Brain Consciousness

1. Jill Bolte Taylor. "My stroke of insight." TED Talk. http:// www.ted.com:80/talks/jill_bolte_taylor_s_powerful_stroke _of_insight.

2. One of the most significant books, perhaps the most significant to date, concerning how and why the two sides of

the brain are different is McGilchrist, I. (2009). *The Master and His Emissary: The Divided Brain and the Making of the Western World.* Yale University Press.

3. The original study on the What and Where pathways is Mishkin, M., and Ungerleider, L. (1982). "Contribution of striate inputs to the visuospatial functions of parieto-preoccipital cortex in monkeys." *Behavioral Brain Research.* 6 (1): 57–77. More recent work on the What and Where system using visual illusions include Goodale, M.A., and Milner, A.D. (1992). "Separate visual pathways for perception and action." *Trends in Neuroscience* 15(1): 20–5; Milner, A. D., and Goodale, M. A. (1995). *The Visual Brain in Action.* Oxford: Oxford University Press.

4. Csikszentmihalyi, M. (1990). *Flow: The Psychology of Optimal Experience.* Harper & Row.

5. Ramachandran, V. S., and Blakeslee, S. (1998). *Phantoms in the Brain.* New York: William Morrow and Company.

Chapter 5: Meaning and Understanding

1. Klein, M. (1981). "Context and memory." In L. T. Benjamin Jr. and K. D. Lowman (eds.), *Activities Handbook for the Teaching of Psychology* (p. 83). Washington, DC: American Psychological Association.

2. The original work on "chunking" and short-term memory is Miller, G. A. (1956). "The magical number seven, plus or minus two: Some limits on our capacity for processing information." *Psychological Review* 63: 81–97.

3. One of the original papers on how deep, meaningful processing affects memory is Craik, F. I. M., and Tulving,

E. (1975). "Depth of processing and the retention of words in episodic memory." *Journal of Experimental Psychology: General* 104: 268–294.

4. Frankl, V. (2006). *Man's Search for Meaning*. Pocket Books.

5. Schooler J. W., Ariely D., and Loewenstein, G. (2003). "The pursuit and assessment of happiness may be self-defeating." In J. Carrilo and I. Brocas (eds.). *The Psychology of Economic Decisions*. Oxford: Oxford University Press, pp. 41–70. Of course if you are trying to be happy, you could never really experience music or anything else that could cause pleasure.

6. Mauss, I. B., et al. (2011). "Can seeking happiness make people unhappy? Paradoxical effects of valuing happiness." *Emotion* 11: 807. This work viewed happiness as an excess of positive emotions; it should be obvious that this is different from meaning.

7. Yang, J. (2014). "The role of the right hemisphere in metaphor comprehension: A meta-analysis of functional magnetic resonance imaging studies." *Human Brain Mapping* 35. 10.1002/hbm.22160.

8. Kozak, A. (2016). *Wild Chickens and Petty Tyrants: 108 Metaphors for Mindfulness*. Wisdom Publications.

9. Mitchell, E. (2008). *The Way of the Explorer, Revised Edition: An Apollo Astronaut's Journey Through the Material and Mystical Worlds*. New Page Books.

Chapter 6: Right-Brain Intelligence—
Intuition, Emotions, and Creativity

1. James, W. (originally published 1890; reprinted in 1950). *The Principles of Psychology*. New York: Dover.

2. Mangan introduced the idea that the fringe represents the big picture, which is too big for typical consciousness. See Mangan, B. (2001). "Sensation's ghost: The non-sensory 'fringe' of consciousness." *PSYCHE* 7(18). http://psyche .cs.monash.edu.au/v7/psyche-7-18-mangan.html.

3. Maril, A., Simons, J. S., Weaver, J. J., and Schacter, D. L. (2005). "Graded recall success: An event-related fMRI comparison of tip of the tongue and feeling of knowing." *NeuroImage* 24(4): 1130–1138.

4. https://www.psychologytoday.com/us/blog/radical -remission/201405/the-science-behind-intuition.

5. Bechara, Antoine, Damasio, Hanna, Tranel, Daniel, and Damasio, Antonio R. "Deciding advantageously before knowing the advantageous strategy." *Science*; Vol. 275, Iss. 5304 (Feb. 28, 1997): 1293–1295.

6. https://www.psychologicalscience.org/news/minds -business/intuition-its-more-than-a-feeling.html.

7. Lufityanto, G., Donkin, C., and Pearson, J. "Measuring intuition: nonconscious emotional information boosts deci-sion accuracy and confidence." *Psychological Science*. https:// doi.org/10.1177/0956797616629403.

8. In the experiment they showed the photos to the right eye or left brain, but of course these were not split-brain patients, so the information could be passed from one side to

the other. It would be interesting to run this experiment on split-brain patients and see if the results would be the same.

9. Goleman, D. (1995). *Emotional Intelligence: Why It Can Matter More Than IQ*. New York: Bantam Books.

10. Goleman, D. (2011). *The Brain and Emotional Intelligence: New Insights*. Florence, MA. More Than Sound.

11. Niebauer, C. (2004). "Handedness and the fringe of consciousness: Strong handers ruminate while mixed handers self-reflect." *Consciousness and Cognition* 13: 730–745. 10.1016/j.concog.2004.07.003.

12. Olatunji, B. O., Lohr, J. M., and Bushman, B. J. (2007). "The pseudopsychology of Venting in the treatment of anger: Implications and alternatives for mental health practice." In T. A. Cavell and K. T. Malcolm (eds.), *Anger, Aggression and Interventions for Interpersonal Violence* (pp. 119–41). Mahwah, NJ, US: Lawrence Erlbaum Associates Publishers. In this chapter the authors state that "In study after study, the conclusion was the same: Expressing anger does not reduce aggressive tendencies and likely makes it worse."

13. Zahn, R., Moll, J., Paiva, M., Garrido, G., Krueger, Fl, Huey, E., et al. (2008). "The neural basis of human social values: evidence from functional MRI." *Cerebral Cortex.* 19: 276–283.

14. Although not all studies on gratitude have told a simple story about greater right-brain activity, one that does is Zahn, R., Garrido, G., Moll, J., and Grafman, J. (2014). "Individual differences in posterior cortical volume correlate with proneness to pride and gratitude." *Social Cognitive and Affective Neuroscience.* 9: 1676–1683.

15. Emmons, R. A., and McCullough, M. E. (2003). "Counting blessings versus burdens: An experimental investigation of gratitude and subjective well-being in daily life." *Journal of Personality and Social Psychology* 84(2): 377–389. This is a very important experiment on gratitude as an actual experiment on the effects of practicing gratitude rather than complaining. To quote the authors, "Results suggest that a conscious focus on blessings may have emotional and interpersonal benefits."

16. Sacks, O. (2015). *Gratitude*. Knopf.

17. "How we read each other's minds," Rebecca Saxe at TEDGlobal 2009. https://www.ted.com/talks /rebecca_saxe_how_brains_make_moral_judgments?utm _campaign=tedspread--a&utm_medium=referral&utm _source=tedcomshare. A more detailed article reviewing her work is Saxe, R. (2010). "The right temporo-parietal junction: A specific brain region for thinking about thoughts." In Alan Leslie and Tamsin German (eds.) *Handbook of Theory of Mind*.

18. Goleman, D. (2011). *The Brain and Emotional Intelligence: New Insights*. Florence, MA. More Than Sound.

19. Mednick, S. A., and Mednick, M. T. (1967). *Examiner's Manual: Remote Associates Test*. Boston: Houghton Mifflin.

20. Bradbury, R. and Aggelis, S. L. (2004). *Conversations with Ray Bradbury*. University Press of Mississippi.

21. Lynch, D. Interview with Andy Battaglia, film.avclub .com. January 23, 2007.

22. Kahneman, D., and Tversky, A. (1972). "Subjective probability: A judgment of representativeness." *Cognitive Psychology* 3(3): 430–454. doi:10.1016/0010 -0285(72)90016-3; Tversky, A., and Kahneman, D. (1974). "Judgment under Uncertainty: Heuristics and Biases." *Science* 185(4157): 1124–1131. doi:10.1126 /science.185.4157.1124. PMID 17835457.

23. Dijksterhuis, A., Bos, M. W., Nordgren, L. F., van Baaren, R. B. (2006). "On making the right choice: the deliberation-without-attention effect." https://www.ncbi. nlm.nih.gov/pubmed/16484496.

Chapter 7: What Is Consciousness?

1. Sheldrake, R. (1988). *The Presence of the Past: Morphic Resonance and the Habits of Nature*. New York: Times Books.

2. Sheldrake, R. (2003). *The Sense of Being Stared At: And Other Aspects of the Extended Mind*. New York: Crown Publishers.

3. Sheldrake, R. (1999). *Dogs That Know When Their Owners Are Coming Home: And Other Unexplained Powers of Animals*. New York: Crown.

4. https://www.newsweek.com/2015/11/20/meet-former -pentagon-scientist-who-says-psychics-can-help-american -spies-393004.html.

5. Botvinick, M., and Cohen, J. (1998). "Rubber hands 'feel' touch that eye sees." *Nature* 391: 756. 10.1038/35784.

6. Ramachandran, V. S., and Altschuler, E. L. (2009). "The use of visual feedback, in particular mirror visual feedback,

in restoring brain function." *Brain* Vol. 132, Issue 7: 1693–1710. https://doi.org/10.1093/brain/awp135.

7. For a more scientific look at this phenomenon, psychologist Daryl Bem did a series of well-controlled experiments and found that people could predict what was going to come up on a computer screen. See https://slate.com/health-and-science/2017/06/daryl-bem-proved-esp-is-real-showed-science-is-broken.html or http://news.cornell.edu/stories/2010/12/study-looks-brains-ability-see-future.

Acknowledgments

I would like to thank my wife Janie, my son Nick, and my daughter Zoe for always encouraging me to follow my right-brain bliss. I would also like to thank everyone at Hierophant Publishing, as their presence can be felt throughout this book. In particular, I would like to thank Randy Davila, as his intuition and wisdom were invaluable during the book creation process. I would also like to thank the following for their help during this adventure: Ben Knight (Zen Ben), Lara Patriquin, Rob Smith, Janet Lee McKnight, Bill Roman, Gary Clise, Christy Homerski, Steve Christman, Shad Connelly and Josh Hudson.

About the Author

Chris Niebauer earned his Ph.D. in Cognitive Neuropsychology at the University of Toledo specializing in differences between the left and right sides of the human brain. He is currently a professor at Slippery Rock University in Pennsylvania, where he teaches courses on consciousness, mindfulness, left- and right-brain differences, and a course on artificial intelligence.

Hierophant Publishing
8301 Broadway, Suite 219
San Antonio, TX 78209
888-800-4240

www.hierophantpublishing.com